Wind Sand and Stars

Antoine de Saint-Exupéry was born into an old French family in 1900. Despite his father's death in 1904 he had an idyllic childhood, shared with his brother and three sisters at the family's château near Lyon. He was educated at a strict Jesuit school in Le Mans and then at the college of Saint-Jean in Fribourg. Against the wishes of his family he qualified as a pilot during his national service, and flew in France and North Africa until his demobilization in 1923. Unsuited to civilian life and deeply hurt by a failed relationship with the writer Louise de Vilmorin, he returned to his first love, flying. In 1926 he joined the airline Latécoère, later to become Aéropostale, as one of its pioneering aviators, charged with opening mail routes to remote African colonies and to South America with primitive planes and in dangerous conditions. As airfield manager at the tiny outpost of Cape Juby in Morocco his duties included rescuing stranded pilots from rebel tribesmen, and it was there that he wrote *Southern Mail*, which was well received on its publication in 1928. From a later posting to Buenos Aires he brought the manuscript of *Night Flight* back to France, together with his fiancée, the beautiful but temperamental Consuelo Suncin. *Night Flight* was awarded the Prix Femina in 1931, firmly establishing his literary reputation. Flying and writing were inseparable elements in his passionate creativity, but he was not a model pilot; he was nonchalant about checks, and tended to lapse into reveries at the controls. His career was chequered with near-fatal crashes and on 30 January 1935 he came down in the Libyan desert while attempting to break the Paris–Saigon record. The story of his miraculous survival is told in *Wind, Sand and Stars*. At the outbreak of the Second World War he was too old to fly a fighter but flew in a reconnaissance squadron until the French surrender in the summer of 1940. In exile in America he wrote the essay *Letter to a Hostage* and *The Little Prince*, the enigmatic children's fable for which he is known worldwide. Prior to this he had written of his war experiences in *Flight to Arras*, which headed the US best-seller list for six months in 1942 and was banned by the Vichy government in France. However, he refused to support de Gaulle and as a result was vilified by the General's Free French supporters. Depressed by this and by his troubled marriage, he persuaded Allied commanders in the Mediterranean to let him fly again, and it was in July 1944 that he disappeared, almost certainly shot down over the sea by a German fighter.

William Rees grew up in Swansea and was educated at the Bishop Gore Grammar School. After graduating from UCW Aberystwyth he continued his studies in French literature and theatre at the University of Exeter and then at St Catherine's College, Oxford. Since 1975 he has taught French and Theatre Studies at Eton College, where he is a House Master. In 1990 he published *The Penguin Book of French Poetry, 1820–1950*, a comprehensive critical anthology with prose translations. His translation of Antoine de Saint-Exupéry's *Flight to Arras* is also published by Penguin.

ANTOINE DE SAINT-EXUPÉRY

Wind, Sand and Stars

*Translated and with an Introduction
by William Rees*

PENGUIN BOOKS

PENGUIN CLASSICS

Published by the Penguin Group
Penguin Books Ltd, 80 Strand, London WC2R 0RL, England
Penguin Group (USA) Inc., 375 Hudson Street, New York, New York 10014, USA
Penguin Group (Canada), 90 Eglinton Avenue East, Suite 700, Toronto, Ontario, Canada M4P 2Y3
(a division of Pearson Penguin Canada Inc.)
Penguin Ireland, 25 St Stephen's Green, Dublin 2, Ireland (a division of Penguin Books Ltd)
Penguin Group (Australia), 250 Camberwell Road, Camberwell, Victoria 3124, Australia
(a division of Pearson Australia Group Pty Ltd)
Penguin Books India Pvt Ltd, 11 Community Centre, Panchsheel Park, New Delhi – 110 017, India
Penguin Group (NZ), 67 Apollo Drive, Rosedale, North Shore 0632, New Zealand
(a division of Pearson New Zealand Ltd)
Penguin Books (South Africa) (Pty) Ltd, 24 Sturdee Avenue,
Rosebank, Johannesburg 2196, South Africa

Penguin Books Ltd, Registered Offices: 80 Strand, London WC2R 0RL, England

www.penguin.com

First published as *Terre des hommes* 1939
This translation first published in Penguin Books 1995
Reprinted in Penguin Classics 2000

11

Translation and introduction copyright © William Rees, 1995
All rights reserved
The moral right of the translator has been asserted

Typeset by Datix International Limited, Bungay, Suffolk
Printed in England by Clays Ltd, St Ives plc
Filmset in Monophoto Garamond

ISBN: 978-0-141-18319-0

www.greenpenguin.co.uk

Penguin Books is committed to a sustainable future
for our business, our readers and our planet.
The book in your hands is made from paper
certified by the Forest Stewardship Council.

CONTENTS

INTRODUCTION

The heroic aviator and prize-winning author Antoine de Saint-Exupéry died at the controls of his plane on 31 July 1944. No body or wreckage was ever found, and the details remain unclear. Suicide was even suggested, for he had been acutely depressed at times in the preceding months, but it is almost certain that he was shot down by a German fighter and crashed into the sea somewhere in the Baie des Anges, between Nice and Monaco. He was returning from a reconnaissance flight undertaken when officially he was grounded, and he was almost certainly off his authorized course and below his planned height after taking nostalgic detours over childhood homes. A massively-built man hampered by old injuries and jammed uncomfortably into his cockpit, his visibility restricted, he may never have seen his attacker; but he was indifferent to danger, for he had confronted death closely many times before, and had come to terms with it physically, intellectually and spiritually. In the absence of radio contact and as his fuel time ran out, those waiting at the base in Corsica knew only that he had disappeared. In the same way Saint-Exupéry himself, back in the pioneering years in Africa and South America, had waited for pilot comrades and then understood that they would never return.

The manner of his death could not fail to augment the mythology that already surrounded this remarkable and complex man whose minutely crafted distillation of experience into epic, lyrical and meditative prose enthralled his generation, and in whom the worlds of childhood and adulthood were never reconciled.

As a pioneering young flier Saint-Exupéry had been driven by a Nietzschean search for fulfilment through self-surpassing adventure. Mature reflection developed in him a humanistic ideal of individual freedom shaped by social and spiritual roots and ennobled by a sense of duty towards all men; the realization of that ideal would lead us to a fraternity in the full achievement of human potential. His vision was coupled with disgust at its antithesis in the increasingly totalitarian 'anthill' of European life in the 1930s.

Yet he was also a man profoundly wounded by the rupturing of the bonds of a blissful childhood. Tortured in his adult relationships with women yet in need of protective feminine love, uncomfortable in the society salons to which his aristocratic name gave him access, he was in his element only in the world of aviation, bantering with mechanics alarmed at his nonchalant technique or sharing the classless camaraderie of his pilot colleagues. At a deeper level, he found in the company of those pilots a mutual, largely unspoken trust and an integrity based on shared experience of adversity, and in their courage and dignity he found his ethical models and his security. When away from that brotherhood he was adrift, at odds with himself and the world, and drawn back fatally towards the inaccessible paradise of childhood.

Antoine ('Tonio' to his family and 'Saint-Ex' to almost everyone in his adult life) was born in Lyon on 29 June 1900. He was the third of five children, but the first son and thus the heir. The family left their elegant town house in the Place Bellecour four years later after the sudden death of Antoine's father, Comte Jean de Saint-Exupéry. They moved to the château of Jean's aunt, the Comtesse de Tricaud, at Saint-Maurice-de-Remens (north-east of Lyon), but also spent a good deal of time at another château near Saint-Tropez; this was La Môle, home of Antoine's maternal grandmother. The autocratic and traditionalist Mme de Tricaud was the dominant figure in family affairs, creating an atmosphere in which only reactionary Catholic and royalist views were acceptable. Antoine was to liberate himself in time from this influence, which was never as powerful as that of his mother, Marie, who developed her son's literary and aesthetic sensibilities and encouraged his imaginative nature. The bond between them was to remain intense in Antoine's later life; her sympathy, approval and love were indispensable to him in his periods of uncertainty and depression, self-criticism and nostalgia.

It was a happy, protected upbringing in a privileged environment which encouraged creativity, though in his later admiration for certain colleagues (notably the calmly heroic flyer Guillaumet and the uncompromising operational director Daurat) we might find the implied absence of a male role model in childhood. Antoine's imagination was given free rein in the double garden paradise of the two châteaux, where he and his brother and sisters transformed the woods and parklands into a magical and limitless kingdom with its own laws and legends. He wrote poetry, stories and plays, and his family had to listen to many hours of reading and performance; he was to make even more extreme demands on his friends as an adult writer in need of constant reassurance and encouragement.

His creative intelligence was also stimulated by mechanical and mathematical challenges, and from an early age he showed the spirit of the aeronautical inventor and designer he was to become in the 1930s, when he patented a number of navigational and landing instruments. At the age of nine he shared in the surge of French pride and enthusiasm when Blériot flew the Channel, and in the national craze for aviation that followed. To his delight (and his mother's anxiety), an airfield and pilot-training school were established close to Saint-Maurice, and the young Antoine spent many hours there watching the fliers and mechanics and absorbing the atmosphere. His dream reached its first fulfilment when one of the pilots took him for a short flight in 1912; tradition has it that it was the 'ace' Védrines, the world speed record holder at the time, but in reality it was almost certainly one of the Salvez brothers, passionate plane-builders who were to die in a crash at the same field two years later.

Though he was able to rediscover it intermittently during holidays, Antoine had been abruptly removed from the garden paradise in 1909 and sent to an austere Jesuit school at Le Mans. The contrast could not have been more harsh, and he never adjusted successfully to the punitive atmosphere and the muscular right-wing ethos of Notre-Dame de Sainte-Croix, which saw itself as a bastion of traditional values in a country falling into decadent republicanism. A number of Antoine's contemporaries later became pro-Nazi and vigorously anti-Semitic; he, on the other hand, came to develop warm friendships with Jews and to open himself generously to other religious cultures, notably Islam.

He neither worked hard nor behaved well at Le Mans, unsurprisingly. He was sulky and abrasive, had no close friends, and received little sympathy from his 'old-school' paternal grandfather with whom he lodged. The only relief came with his mother's periodic visits, though her disagreements with her father-in-law over Antoine's experience at school gave him a troubled insight into the confused expectations of adult life.

In 1915, when his mother was nursing wounded soldiers, he was moved to the Marist school at Fribourg in Switzerland. This was a happier experience at a more tolerant and progressive establishment, but the period was scarred for ever in his memory by the death of his brother François. The manner of that death and of the two boys' last conversation was extraordinary and moving, and it enters naturally into the narrative of *Flight to Arras* when Saint-Ex, facing death himself, discovers his own indifference to his physical body as his brother had done twenty-four years earlier.

His intermittent experience of Parisian life began in 1917, when he was sent to the Lycée Saint-Louis to prepare for the examination to enter the Naval academy. But his heart was never in it. Still depressed after his brother's death, he began to roam aristocratic social circles as a would-be writer, made an abortive fresh start in architecture, fretted about his non-involvement in the war and dreamed of flying. This shapeless period seemed to end positively in 1918 with a decision to join the army and seek an immediate transfer to pilot training, but the war ended before he could put the plan into practice. Haunted by what he saw as a failure to fight, he made a half-hearted and unsuccessful attempt at the Naval examination in 1919.

The following year, however, brought a change in prospects: he was called up for military service and joined a fighter unit at Strasbourg as a mechanic. With one foot inside the door of aviation but unqualified for the officers' flight-training school, he pestered his reluctant mother until she sent him money for private flying lessons. He survived a bad landing and engine fire on his first solo flight, and pressed on with enthusiasm; the characteristic tone of his eventful flying career was set. He circumvented the mainland system by qualifying as a military pilot in Morocco, and after a period of officer-training in 1922 he was posted to a fighter squadron at Le Bourget, but early in 1923 he suffered a fractured skull in a crash.

His career as a pilot was in the balance, and the opposition of his own relatives was now matched by the disapproval of the family of Louise de Vilmorin, with whom he had fallen deeply in love. He was for a time engaged to this elegant, wealthy socialite and writer, but she seems to have taken the relationship much less seriously than the tormented Antoine, who was deeply wounded by its eventual failure and drew extensively on the experience in the composition of his first full-length work, the novel *Southern Mail* (*Courrier sud*, 1928).

Louise was a talented writer, a brilliant conversationalist, a beautiful and flirtatious woman always surrounded by admirers, inseparably wedded to the chic Parisian literary world and quite incapable of following Saint-Ex to the ends of the earth where he dreamed of flying. She found him impossibly intense and demanding, and their temperaments were so incompatible that the relationship's failure was inevitable, even though he withdrew from the air force for her sake and took a series of mundane and frustrating civilian jobs. Astonishingly, the wife he was to bring back from South America eight years later was by temperament an extreme, less controlled version of Louise, and the marriage was a stormy one. No woman could ever match for Antoine the devotion of his mother, but he made strange and impetuous choices in his search for a loving partner who would be prepared to submit her needs to his dangerous career and his emotionally demanding nature.

But the unhappy 1923–6 period was highly productive in a literary sense, for he spent a great deal of time working to refine his style and establishing contacts in the publishing world. It was increasingly clear to him and to his friends that his flying and his writing were mutually nourishing, and indeed that they were inseparable aspects of his creativity. The year 1926 thus brought a happy conjunction, with the publication of his story *L'Aviateur* (effectively a sketch for *Courrier sud*) and his employment by the Latécoère airline company, which was opening up airmail routes into Africa and South America. Antoine found in Latécoère, at last, his true métier and milieu; despite the dangers of the work, and in a sense because of those dangers, the next five years were to be the happiest and most secure of his life after his exile from the magical domain of childhood.

Latécoère, later known as Aéropostale, was a pioneering company of airborne adventurers. It was created by Pierre-Georges Latécoère, a former munitions manufacturer, and driven forward despite immense practical difficulties and considerable loss of life by its operational director, Didier Daurat. Some saw Daurat as a cold and ruthless man, but for Saint-Ex he was an exemplary leader, carrying out his difficult role with wisdom and with a courageous resolve that amounted to an unspoken but inspiring ethical idealism. For the inexperienced young pilot, surrounded by war-hardened veterans who responded to Daurat's leadership, his integrity was the model in their battle with the elements. Those were the days of flimsy planes, unreliable engines, open cockpits and fallible navigational equipment; often there was no radio communication, and maps were poor. By 1930, when the whole route from France to Chile was finally established, over 120 Latécoère employees and passengers were dead, but they had played their part in creating the global village that we now take for granted; whatever his nature and methods, Daurat must indeed have been an inspiring leader.

It would be reductive and simplistic to see the character Rivière in *Night Flight* (*Vol de nuit*, Saint-Exupéry's second novel, published in 1931) purely as a portrait of Daurat, but there is no doubt that the real man largely inhabits the fictional figure. Rivière is seen by some as reminiscent of Corneille's tragic heroes in his ennobling experience of painful paradox and his implied ethic of self-creation through adversity within the sublime torment of early night flying. Daurat, a decisive man of action, certainly exercised a significant influence on the evolution of Saint-Exupéry's thought.

For Saint-Ex those five years were a golden age of comradeship and professional discipline, of confident self-definition through action transmuted into words, of pride in himself and in the classless elite of selfless heroes around him. It was a time of fulfilment through duty in the tenacious struggle with the Sahara and the Andes, harsh environments in which a man could test himself to the limits and which he came in time to love. Those Promethean years are evoked with a remarkable poetic power in *Wind, Sand and Stars* (*Terre des hommes*, 1939). In this book he broke with fiction and wrote in the first person, but in a distilled and non-linear form that defies genre classification and relates all concrete experience to transcendent human values, while remaining essentially a gripping adventure story. The poet Léon-Paul Fargue, his friend, would have called it 'poetic alchemy'. The book is in fact a reworked collection of disparate articles and stories with a unifying spirit of evolving humanism. André Gide had seen the potential for it in the earlier autobiographical fiction, and encouraged Saint-Exupéry to compose, at a distance of a decade or more, this lyrical and absorbing synthesis of a five-year experience. Filled with heightened perceptions of the world and of men, it becomes a celebration of life and of human potential.

He was to recapture the spirit of that camaraderie at the edge of human experience in his reconnaissance squadron in 1940, even in the chaos and wretchedness of the French defeat. In the course of *Flight to Arras* (*Pilote de guerre*, 1942) it is one of the factors which help him to animate within himself a resurgence of human dignity and the will to resist oppression, without vindictiveness towards the cowards, incompetents and bystanders who have allowed the disaster to happen.

The reality of his time with Latécoère was of course not always as ennobling as its poeticized evocation in *Wind, Sand and Stars* might suggest. There was loneliness, and boredom, and limitless sand; there was life in a primitive hut at Cape Juby (now Tarfaya) in the western Sahara as the company's representative, negotiating laboriously with the local Spanish garrison and with Arab tribesmen who had not yet acquired the nobility of spirit conferred on them in the book; there was bureaucracy, and waiting, and foul weather. But all of that is obliterated by the literary memory or passed through a creative filtering process, and the finest times in those five years are synthesized into a story of heroic flights and rescues, magical encounters and elemental, transforming experiences in the desert and the Andes – and so much the better, for *Wind, Sand and Stars* is a magnificently crafted prose poem, not a report. An essence, not a log-book. The transcendent significance of men, machines, objects and landscapes burns as fiercely and generously in the work of this master of concise metaphorical analogy as it does in the best Symbolist poetry.

Saint-Ex flew sections of the north and west Africa mail routes, dicing frequently with death in storms and forced landings, or at the hands of tribesmen in revolt against the competitive Franco-Spanish colonization of their territories. In 1929, he was transferred to Buenos Aires, where in addition to flying duties he exercised administrative responsibility (rather reluctantly) for the establishment of the last southern section, through Patagonia to the southern tip of the continent at Punta Arenas. His experiences at the airfields and in the stormy skies of South America generated *Night Flight* and the remarkable section of *Wind, Sand and Stars* which recounts, in an understated form appropriate to the man, Guillaumet's almost unbelievable walk to safety after a crash landing in a high Andean storm – a survival which was later to inspire and guide Saint-Ex through his own parallel experience in the Libyan desert.

1931 was a watershed year of a largely negative kind, despite the award of the Prix Femina for *Night Flight* (bestowed by an entirely female jury on a writer whose works might be thought conventionally to exist in a distinctly masculine realm). It was a best-seller, and applications for pilot-training doubled in the following year. But as he gained literary fame Saint-Exupéry's life was changing. He would never be consistently happy again, despite his continuing capacity for bursts of spontaneous joy, playfulness and affection. The company was breaking up under financial pressure and in an atmosphere of rancour, and it was eventually absorbed by an unsympathetic government into the new Air France conglomerate. That represented for Saint-Ex the dispiriting end of an ideal enterprise, and now his emotional life was intensely complicated following his marriage to Consuelo Suncin, the beautiful but wildly temperamental widow he had met in Buenos Aires. An initially passionate mutual fascination concealed a fundamental incompatibility of aspirations of the kind Saint-Ex had already experienced with Louise de Vilmorin. In the years that followed, their volatile natures clashed more often than they blended and they were apart as often as they were together, though there is no doubt that they loved each other deeply. He wrote her frequent, anguished letters during their separations, and she is the model for the Rose in *The Little Prince*.

The 1930s were unsettled, disordered years. The sale of the

château at Saint-Maurice was distressing, and there were frequent changes of address and money troubles often connected with the couple's marital problems. As Aéropostale collapsed amid factional disputes there were wounding, artistically immobilizing criticisms from some former comrades who objected to his portrayal of Daurat and felt that he had exploited their painful experiences for commercial gain. The critics did not include Guillaumet and Mermoz, the two comrades for whom he had the greatest admiration and respect, but those attacks probably played a part in his move away from narrative fiction.

His flying activities became more intermittent and included several serious crashes: he almost drowned in 1932 when he capsized a seaplane he was testing; early in 1936 came the miraculous survival in the Libyan desert that forms the climax and the crux of *Wind, Sand and Stars*; and in 1938, attempting a pioneering long-distance flight from New York to Tierra del Fuego, he suffered multiple fractures and severe concussion when his plane came down in Guatemala. He also undertook promotional tours for Air France, gave lectures, patented inventions, performed flying sequences for a film version of *Southern Mail*, observed Nazism at its height in Germany (where he was briefly arrested on suspicion of spying), and travelled to Russia and to the Spanish Civil War front as a reporter. From the Russian journey he drew the poignant account of the Polish emigrant workers which became the coda of *Terre des hommes*, and from Spain he absorbed new examples of human generosity and dignity in self-sacrifice. The publication of that work in 1939 was a triumph, bringing him the supreme accolade of the Grand Prix du Roman de l'Académie.

Terre des hommes was and remains a genuinely popular book in France, inspirational in the days of the Nazi Occupation and ranked among the best-selling books of the century. Yet in several ways it seemed to form an anachronistic climax to a decade in which the heady days of open cockpits were past, and in which its author had become more meditative, less concrete and more moralistic in the notes he was composing for future publication as *Citadelle*. He had grown more emotionally fragile, more tormented by self-analysis and by nostalgia for the innocent freedom of childhood, and yet also more than ever convinced of a fundamental human dignity, brotherhood and innate creativity existing beyond the mediocrity of modern urban life. Despite the rise of Fascism in that decade and the imminence of a terrible war, he remained certain that human solidarity was the only true wealth in life, mutual responsibility the only ethic.

In July 1939, Saint-Ex was aboard as an observer when his old friend and mentor Guillaumet broke the transatlantic seaplane record. In August, he hurried back to France as war became inevitable. Because of his age and his injuries Saint-Ex was declared unfit for active service and assigned to technical instruction, but meek acceptance of that would have been out of character. After some frustrations he was eventually posted to 2/33 Reconnaissance Squadron, where he enjoyed a rebirth of the old spirit of camaraderie in a sacred duty, even though 'everything was falling apart' as France crumbled before the Nazi tanks and old friends died (including Guillaumet). His experience at 2/33 – above all his mission on 22 May 1940 – forms the narrative and philosophical substance of *Flight to Arras*. As he recounts the mission he progresses from initial bitterness at its futility, through an extraordinary survival under intense shellfire, to a homeward journey in which he reaches a profound state of insight into himself, his defeated country and its people, the causes of its isolation and the seeds of its regeneration

In 1942, the book was published almost simultaneously in France and in the USA, where Saint-Ex was living in exile. It had an immense impact in both countries: the German censors banned it in France the following year because of the lucid patriotism and the inspiration to Resistance which its closing chapters embodied, together with its provocative eulogy of the Jewish pilot Israel. In America it headed the best-seller list for six months as the country was committing itself to the war against Germany and Japan. *Flight to Arras* was the first book to seek a resolution of shameful paradoxes, to draw sense out of chaos and truth out of error, and to bring a phoenix of national pride and hope out of the débâcle of 1940. However rhetorical its closing chapters may seem now (a foretaste of *Citadelle*), there is no doubt that it played a significant role in restoring respect for France and in strengthening public opinion behind American involvement in the liberation of Europe.

How ironic and unfortunate it was, then, that Saint-Exupéry's position with regard to the collaborationist Vichy government and de Gaulle's Free French forces subsequently became blurred to the point where the latter also banned *Pilote de guerre*. In addition to his contempt for extremist ideologies of right and left, he had always stood aloof from French politicians, viewing them as self-seeking, scheming mediocrities who did not have the true spirit of the nation at heart. He took particular exception to General de Gaulle, and the feeling was mutual. The General seemed to him to be principally interested in establishing the foundations of post-war power for himself and his immediate supporters, and not in the national unity that was so crucial to the country's rebirth. So it was, in part, that after his spectacular flying career and literary success this holder of the Légion d'Honneur and the Croix de Guerre was ostracized and vilified by the Gaullistes, who formed an influential group among the large and quarrelsome community of French intellectuals, politicians and artists in exile in New York.

It is also true, however, that after his disgust at the failures of command of 1939–40 Saint-Exupéry had adopted what seemed a surprisingly pro-Vichy stance. He came to feel that Free French resistance was futile until America could be persuaded to join the war, and that to set Frenchman against Frenchman would bring nothing but disaster to the country and its people. Yet while giving the Pétain administration his provisional and rather tormented support, he was at the same time exploring the possibility of flying for the British RAF.

In 1943, after the publication of *Letter to a Hostage* and *The Little Prince*, the Allied presence in North Africa gave him the definitive opportunity to show where his heart lay. 2/33 Squadron was now in Algeria, flying Lightnings under American command. His age and his medical record were against him, but once again he pestered and pulled strings with extraordinary tenacity until he was given limited permission to fly, and then repeated the process after being grounded following a bad landing. The Squadron moved to Sardinia and then to Corsica as the Liberation of southern France approached, and on 31 July 1944 Saint-Ex took off for that final reconnaissance flight over Annecy and Grenoble.

His great and unfinished project, *Citadelle* (*Wisdom of the Sands*), was published posthumously, as were many of his letters and journals. Begun in 1936 and a huge volume even as it stands, it was to be the fruit of an ethical and spiritual exploration on which he planned to spend ten more years. Filled with parables, it develops the meditative aspect of his earlier books in the mind and the voice of a Berber chieftain, and in a dense, biblically rhetorical style.

Relatively few will have read *Citadelle* in full, but millions world-wide have read *The Little Prince*, which was composed during his troubled exile in America and a last attempt at reconciliation with Consuelo. This original, enigmatic fable (ostensibly for children yet with layers of significance for adults) startled the literary world on its appearance, and is now probably the most widely translated French book. An autobiographical and philosophical allegory, naively fantastical and absorbingly subtle at the same time, it is an exquisite story involving a crashed pilot, a small boy with golden hair who arrives beside him in the desert after an interplanetary journey, a fox, a sheep, a snake and a rose. Illustrated by its author's own water-colours, it is about human bonding, about creativity and the primacy of the heart over the intellect, and about Consuelo; it is also about childhood, adulthood and the loss of innocence.

Saint-Ex's small but superbly crafted and powerfully engaging output has ensured for him a significant place in the literary culture of his century. The context has changed, the machines that are for him an instrument for human growth and not an end in themselves have grown more sophisticated, but his voice still has a place at the end of that century. That voice, in which action and language are one, is still inspirational.

A young officer at 2/33 wrote this in the Squadron diary on the evening of 31 July 1944:

'In him we have lost not only our most valued comrade, but the man who was to us a fine example of faith. If he came to share our dangers in spite of his age, it was not to add vainglory to an already magnificent career, but because he felt within himself the need to do it. Saint-Exupéry is among the greats, those who face life knowing how to respect themselves as men.'

A NOTE ON THE TEXT

The text that follows is a translation of the definitive edition of *Terre des hommes*. It thus differs from Lewis Galantière's version, which has been established since 1939. Galantière convinced Saint-Exupéry of the need for some additional contextual material for American readers, and insisted on retaining some quite extensive passages which the author had removed from the French text in a characteristically ruthless drive for concision and unity. Inexplicably, Galantière then omitted the author's important introductory page.

There is also the question of the title, which is of course not a direct rendering of *Terre des hommes*. Such an aim would have been difficult to accomplish in a felicitous way. I would have enjoyed the challenge, but with some reluctance (and some relief) I must accept not only the fact that Galantière's title is so well established that a change might be confusing and perhaps even offensive, but also the fact that Saint-Exupéry himself agreed to it. So *Wind, Sand and Stars* must stand.

It is certainly time now for this text to be refreshed for English-speaking readers (with Saint-Exupéry's present tense restored), and for it to be given a crisper economy of style which might come closer to the pulse of the original. I hope I have succeeded to some degree in those aims.

I would like to acknowledge the help with linguistic and meteorological obscurities given by my colleagues Delphine Lemonnier, Charlotte Gendron, Jean-Paul Dubois and Michael Town, and to thank my wife and children for their enthusiastic support and critical proofreading.

W. R.

FURTHER READING

Albérès, R. M., *Saint-Exupéry*, Albin Michel, 1961

Albérès, R. M., et al., *Saint-Exupéry*, Collection Génies et Réalités, Hachette, 1963

Cate, C., *Antoine de Saint-Exupéry: His Life and Times*, Heinemann, 1970

Chevrier, P., *Antoine de Saint-Exupéry*, Gallimard, 1949

Destrem, M., *Saint-Exupéry*, Editions Paris-Match, 1974

Estang, L., *Saint-Exupéry*, Seuil, 1956

Fleury, J.-G., *La Ligne de Mermoz, Guillaumet, Saint-Exupéry et leurs compagnons d'épopée*, Gallimard, 1949

Migéo, M., *Saint-Exupéry*, Flammarion, 1958

Schiff, S., *Saint-Exupéry*, Chatto & Windus, 1994

Tavernier, R., et al., *Saint-Exupéry en procès*, Editions Pierre Belford, 1967

Webster, P., *Antoine de Saint-Exupéry: the Life and Death of the Little Prince*, Macmillan, 1993

This book is dedicated to Henri Guillaumet, my comrade.

FOREWORD

The earth teaches us more about ourselves than all the books in the world, because it is resistant to us. Self-discovery comes when man measures himself against an obstacle. To attain it, he needs an implement. He needs a carpenter's plane, or a plough. Little by little, as he walks behind the plough, the farmer forces out a few of nature's secrets, and the truth which he uncovers is universal. In the same way the aeroplane, the implement of the airline companies, brings man face to face with all the old problems.

In my mind's eye I still have the image of my first night flight in Argentina. It was a dark night, with only occasional scattered lights glittering like stars on the plain.

Each one, in that ocean of shadows, was a sign of the miracle of consciousness. In one home people were reading, or thinking, or sharing confidences. In another, perhaps, they were searching through space, wearying themselves with the mathematics of the Andromeda nebula. In another they were making love. These small flames shone far apart in the landscape, demanding their fuel. Even the most unassuming of them, the flame of the poet, the teacher or the carpenter. But among these living stars, how many closed windows, how many extinct stars, how many sleeping men . . .

We must surely seek unity. We must surely seek to communicate with some of those fires burning far apart in the landscape.

I

THE AIRLINE

It was 1926. I had just signed on as a trainee airline pilot with the Latécoère Company, which operated the Toulouse–Dakar route before it was taken over by Aéropostale and later by Air France. I was learning the trade. Like my comrades, I was passing in my turn through the novitiate before being granted the honour of piloting the mail. Air trials, Toulouse–Perpignan shuttles, dismal meteorology classes in a freezing hangar. We lived in fear of the yet unknown Spanish mountains, and in reverence for our elders.

We used to meet those veterans in the canteen. Gruff and a little distant, they passed on their condescending advice. And when one of them came in late after a flight from Alicante or Casablanca, in his rain-soaked leathers, and one of us asked him timid questions about his journey, his terse replies constructed in our minds on those stormy days a fabulous world filled with traps and snares, with cliffs that loom up suddenly and whirling currents that could uproot cedars. Dark dragons guarded the valley gateways, sprays of lightning crowned the mountain crests. In the art of maintaining our reverence those veterans were masters. But from time to time one of them, revered for eternity, did not come back.

I remember one such homecoming. It was old Bury, who died later in the Corbières. He had just sat down at our table, and was eating his food in a leaden silence, his shoulders still hunched from his exertions. It was the end of one of those bad days when the sky is filthy from start to finish of the route, when the pilot's eye sees all the mountains wallowing in slime like loose cannon churning up the deck of an old sailing ship. I gazed at Bury, swallowed hard, and ventured to ask him if it had been a tough flight. Bent over his plate, his brow furrowed, Bury didn't hear me. In bad weather, you had to lean out of those open planes to see anything, and the crashing of the wind went on reverberating long afterwards in your ears. At last Bury raised his head, seemed to hear me and to remember, then burst into ringing laughter. His laughter was a thing of wonder, for he laughed so rarely; it illumined his weariness. He gave no further explanation of his achievement, but lowered his head and went on chewing in silence. But in that colourless dining-room, among humble clerks repairing the petty wear and tear of the day, that heavy-shouldered comrade struck me as having a strange nobility; through his rough hide he had let us glimpse the angel who had vanquished the dragon.

At last came the night when it was my turn to be called to the manager's office. He said, simply, 'You're flying tomorrow.'

I stood motionless, waiting for leave to go. But after a silence he added, 'I take it you know the regulations?'

Engines, at that time, were not safe like today's engines. They would often give up on you without warning, with a great crashing of breaking crockery. And you gave the plane its head towards the rocky crust of Spain which offered precious few refuges. 'Up here,' we used to say, 'when your engine cracks up, your plane isn't far behind.' But a plane can be replaced. The vital thing was not to fly blindly into a rock face, so we were forbidden, under threat of the most severe disciplinary action, to fly over the oceans of cloud above mountainous regions. A pilot in trouble, sinking into the white flax, might crash into a peak without ever seeing it.

That is why a slow voice, that evening, was giving the regulation its full and final weight:

'It's a great thing, flying by the compass over an ocean of Spanish clouds; it's very stylish, but . . .'

And the voice spoke even more deliberately:

'. . . but remember what is under the ocean of clouds: eternity.'

And suddenly that tranquil world, the world of such simple harmony that you discover as you rise above the clouds, took on an unfamiliar quality in my eyes. All that gentleness became a trap. In my mind's eye I saw that vast white trap laid out, right under my feet. Beneath it reigned neither the restlessness of men nor the living tumult and motion of cities, as one might have thought, but a silence that was even more absolute, a more final peace. That viscous whiteness was turning before my eyes into the boundary between the real and the unreal, between the known and the unknowable. And I was already beginning to sense that a spectacle has no meaning except when seen through a culture, a civilization, a professional craft. Mountain people knew the sea of clouds too, and yet they did not see in it this fabulous curtain.

When I left the office I felt a childish pride. My turn had come. At daybreak I would be responsible for a cargo of passengers, and for the African mail. But I also experienced a great sense of humility. I felt unprepared. There were few safe places in Spain; faced with the threat of engine failure, I feared that I would not know where to look for a welcoming emergency field. I had pored over my unrewarding maps, not finding in them the lessons I needed. And so I went, my heart filled with a mix of uncertainty and pride, to spend that knightly vigil with my comrade Guillaumet. Guillaumet had done those routes before me. He knew the tricks of the trade, the ones that opened Spanish locks. I needed to be initiated by Guillaumet.

When I walked in he smiled:

'I've heard the news. Are you pleased?'

He went to the cupboard for glasses and a bottle of port, then turned back towards me, still smiling:

'Let's drink to it. It'll be fine, you'll see.'

He gave off confidence as a lamp gives light, this comrade who was later to break the records for postal crossings of the Andean Cordillera and of the South Atlantic. Some years before that, sitting there that evening in his shirtsleeves, his arms folded in the lamplight, smiling the most heartening of smiles, he said to me simply:

'Sometimes the storms and the fog and the snow will get you down. But think of all those who have been through it before you, and just tell yourself: "They did it, so it can be done again."'

But I unrolled my maps all the same, and asked him to go over the journey with me, just briefly. And in the lamplight, leaning on the veteran's shoulder, I felt a peace unknown since my schooldays.

But what a strange geography lesson I was given! Guillaumet didn't teach me about Spain, he made Spain my friend. He didn't talk about hydrography, or population figures, or livestock. Instead of talking about Guadix, he spoke of three orange trees at the edge of a field near Guadix: 'Watch out for those, mark them on your map . . .' And from then on the three orange trees had more significance than the Sierra Nevada. He didn't talk about Lorca, but about an ordinary farm near Lorca. A living farm, with its farmer and its farmer's wife. And that couple, lost in emptiness a thousand miles away from us, took on an importance beyond measure. Settled there on their mountain slope, they were ready, like lighthouse-keepers under their stars, to give help to men.

From their oblivion, from their inconceivable remoteness we rescued such details, known to no geographer in the world. Only the Ebro, which waters great cities, is of interest to geographers. Not that little stream hidden in the weeds to the west of Motril, that stream that fosters thirty species of flowers. 'Beware of that stream, it ruins the field for landing . . . Mark that on your map too.' Oh, I would remember that snake at Motril! It looked like nothing at all, it enchanted no more than a few frogs with its gentle murmur, but it slept with only one eye closed. In the paradise of that emergency landing-field, it lay in wait for me in the grasses, twelve hundred miles away. Given the chance, it would transform me into a sheaf of flames . . .

And I was braced and ready to meet those thirty fighting sheep, drawn up on the hillside there and ready to charge: 'You think the meadow is clear, and then wham! – you've got thirty sheep running down under your wheels . . .' I could only smile in astonishment at such cunning treachery.

Little by little, in the lamplight, the Spain of my map became a fairytale landscape. I marked with a cross the sanctuaries and the traps. Like beacons I charted the farmer, the thirty sheep, the stream. I pinpointed exactly that shepherdess neglected by the geographers.

When I left Guillaumet, I felt the need to walk in the icy air of that winter night. I turned up my coat collar, and among the oblivious passers-by my youthful fervour walked with me. I was proud to be brushing past those strangers with my secret in my heart. They knew me not, those barbarians, but it was to me that they would be entrusting their anxieties and their passions, come daybreak and the loading of the mailbags. Into my hands they would be delivering up their hopes. Among them then, wrapped in my coat, I walked as a protector, but they knew nothing of my care for them.

Nor were they aware of the messages I was receiving from the night. For my physical being itself was affected by the snowstorm that might be gathering to trouble my first flight. Stars were disappearing one by one, but how could those walkers have known it? I alone was in the secret, receiving the enemy's positions before the battle . . .

And yet those watchwords that involved me so deeply were coming to me as I walked by bright shop windows with their shining Christmas presents. All the world's good things seemed to be displayed there, in the darkness, and I tasted the proud intoxication of renunciation. I was a warrior in danger: what did they matter to me, those shining crystals destined for evenings of celebration, those lampshades, those books? I was already soaked in the spray; an airline pilot now, I was already biting into the bitter pulp of night flight.

When they woke me it was three in the morning. I snapped open the shutters, saw that rain was falling on the town, and dressed solemnly.

The street glistened with rain as I sat on my small suitcase half an hour later, waiting for the bus to pick me up. So many comrades before me, on their ordination day, had experienced this same wait, this tightening of the heart. The antiquated bus appeared at last at the street corner, in a fracas of metallic noise, and now it was my right to squeeze onto the bench between a sleepy customs man and a group of clerks. That bus had a stale smell of dusty bureaucracies, old offices where a man's life sinks into the peat. Every five hundred yards it stopped to take on board another secretary, another customs man, an inspector. Those who were already asleep responded with a vague grunt to the greeting of the newcomer, who squeezed in wherever he could and then dozed off in his turn. It was a mournful cartload that made its way over the uneven cobblestones of Toulouse; and the airline pilot in the midst of those bureaucrats was at first scarcely distinguishable from them . . . But the streetlamps filed by, the airfield drew nearer, and now the rattling old bus had become a grey chrysalis from which that man would emerge transfigured.

Every comrade before me, on such a morning, had sensed a birth taking place within his young man's vulnerability as it endured that inspector's surliness, the birth of the Spanish and African Mail pilot, the birth of the man who in three hours would be confronting the dragon amid the lightning storms of the Hospitalet ... who after his victory in four hours' time would be deciding in complete freedom, and in possession of all his powers, between a detour over the sea and a direct assault on the Alcoy range, and whose dealings were now to be with storm, sea and mountain.

Every comrade before me on such a morning, indistinguishable from that anonymous group beneath the dismal winter sky of Toulouse, had felt the growth within him of that monarch who, five hours later, leaving behind him the rains and snows of the North, repudiating winter, would throttle back his engine and begin his descent through a midsummer sky into the dazzling sunlight of Alicante.

That old bus has disappeared, but its austerity and discomfort still live in my memory. It was a fine symbol of the apprenticeship we had to undergo for the harsh joys of our craft. Within it everything took on a striking seriousness. And I remember that it was in that bus three years later that I learned, though fewer than ten words were spoken, of the death of Lécrivain, one of those hundred colleagues in the company who one foggy day or night retired for eternity.

It was three in the morning then, in the familiar silence. We heard the manager, unseen in the darkness, speaking to the inspector:

'Lécrivain didn't land at Casablanca last night.'

'Oh,' replied the inspector. 'Oh?'

Pulled abruptly from his dream, he made an effort to wake up, to show some earnestness, and added:

'Oh, really? He didn't get through? Did he turn back?'

The answer, from deep at the back of the bus, was simply: 'No.' We waited to hear more, but no words came. And as the seconds fell away, it became clearer that no further word would follow that 'no', that there was no appeal against that 'no', that not only had Lécrivain failed to land at Casablanca, he would never again land anywhere.

And so that morning, at the dawn of my first mail flight, I too underwent the sacred rites of my profession. I felt my confidence failing as I gazed through the windows at the reflections of the streetlamps in the shining tarmac. The wind made great palm leaves that scudded over the surface of the puddles. And I thought: 'My first mail flight . . . honestly . . . just my luck.' I looked up at the inspector:

'Bad weather, do you think?'

The inspector cast a weary gaze through the window:

'Can't tell from this,' he grunted eventually. And I wondered how you recognized bad weather. The previous evening, Guillaumet had effaced with just a smile all the ill omens which the veterans had laid upon us, but now I was remembering them: 'In a snowstorm, I pity the man who doesn't know the whole route pebble by pebble . . . Oh yes, I pity him!' They had to maintain their glamour, and they shook their heads as they looked at us with a rather embarrassing compassion, as if they were pitying our innocent naivety.

And for how many of us already had that bus been a last place of safety? Sixty? Eighty? All driven by the same taciturn driver on a rainy morning. I looked around me: there were points of light in the darkness, as cigarettes punctuated meditation, the humble meditation of ageing clerks. For how many of us had these companions served as a funeral escort?

I overheard their muttered exchanges of confidences, stories of illness, money, sad domestic worries that revealed the dismal prison in which those men had immured themselves. And suddenly I had a vision of the face of destiny.

Old bureaucrat, my companion here present, no man ever opened an escape route for you, and you are not to blame. You built peace for yourself by blocking up every chink of light, as termites do. You rolled yourself into your ball of bourgeois security, your routines, the stifling rituals of your provincial existence, you built your humble rampart against winds and tides and stars. You have

no wish to ponder great questions, you had enough trouble suppress-
ing awareness of your human condition. You do not dwell on a
wandering planet, you ask yourself no unanswerable questions;
lower-middle-class Toulouse, that's you. No man ever grasped you
by the shoulder while there was still time. Now the clay that formed
you has dried and hardened, and no man could now awaken in you
the dormant musician, the poet or the astronomer who perhaps
once dwelt within you.

The squalls of rain no longer trouble me. The magic of my
profession is revealing to me a world where within two hours I
shall confront the dark dragons and the crests crowned with a mane
of blue lightning; and then, set free by the coming of night, I shall
chart my course in the stars.

That was the form of our professional baptism, and we began to fly.
More often than not those flights were uneventful. Like divers, we
sank peacefully into the depths of our domain. Today it has been
thoroughly explored; the pilot, the engineer and the radio operator
aren't embarking on an adventure now, but shutting themselves in
a laboratory. They respond to instrument needles, not to the
unfolding of a landscape. Outside their capsule the mountains are
immersed in darkness, but they are not mountains now. They are
invisible powers whose approach is reckoned mathematically. The
radio operator notes down figures reliably in the lamplight, the
engineer checks the map, and the pilot changes course if the
mountains have drifted a little, if the peaks he meant to pass on the
left have spread themselves before him in the secretive silence of
military manoeuvres.

As for the listening stations on the ground, they take down
reliably, simultaneously, the words dictated by their colleague:
'Midnight forty. Bearing 230. All well on board.'

That is how they fly today, with no sense that they are in motion.
The crew are far from any landmark, as if on the ocean at night. But
the engines fill the lighted cabin with a throbbing that changes its
very nature. The clock moves on. A comprehensive, invisible
alchemy is taking place in those dials, those radio valves, those
pointers. Moment by moment, those arcane gestures, those muffled
words and that concentration are preparing the miracle. And when

the hour has come, the pilot can press his forehead against the screen in perfect confidence. Gold has been born out of Nothingness: it shines in the lights of the airfield.

And yet we have all known flights when suddenly, in the light of a particular perspective, two hours out, each of us has felt our remoteness as we would not have felt it in the Indies, a remoteness beyond hope of homecoming.

So it was when Mermoz made the first seaplane crossing of the South Atlantic. As the daylight was dying he came into the Doldrums.[1] Moment by moment he watched as the tornadoes tied their tails together before him, as if a wall were taking shape. Then darkness fell, drawing a curtain on this prologue. When he slipped below the clouds an hour later, he entered a fantastical kingdom.

Waterspouts stood in apparently motionless ranks like the pillars of a temple. On their swollen capitals rested the dark and lowering arch of the storm, but blades of light sliced down through cracks in the arch, and between the pillars the full moon gleamed on the cold stone tiles of the sea. And Mermoz made his way through those empty ruins, banking for four hours from one channel of light to another, circling round those giant pillars with the sea surely surging up inside them, following those flows of moonlight towards the exit from the temple. And this spectacle was so overwhelming that Mermoz, once through the Doldrums, realized that he had not been afraid.

I too remember one of those moments when you pass beyond the borders of the real world: the radio direction finders transmitting from the Sahara airfields had been wrong all night, and had sent me and my radiotelegrapher Néri seriously off course. When suddenly I saw the gleam of water at the bottom of a crevasse in the fog, I turned sharply in the direction of the coast; we had no idea how long we had been flying out towards the open sea.

The coast was perhaps out of reach, for our fuel could well run out. Even if we made the coast we still had to find the airfield. And now the moon was setting. With no angular orientation and already

---

[1]Doldrums: often thought of as an area of flat calm, but in fact also subject to violent storms and updraughts.

deaf, we were becoming progressively blind. The moon was fading to nothing, like a pallid ember, in a fog that resembled a snowdrift. The sky above us too was filling with clouds, and we flew on and on between cloud and fog, in a world void of all light and of all substance.

The airfields that answered us gave up telling us what we knew: 'No bearings . . . No bearings . . .' for our voice was coming to them from everywhere and nowhere.

And suddenly, when we had begun to despair, a shining point of light revealed itself on the horizon, ahead of us to port. I felt a surge of joy. Néri leaned towards me, and I heard him singing! What could it be but the airfield beacon, for at night the Sahara, black in its entirety, is a vast dead territory. But the light flickered for a moment, then went out. We had set our course for a star, visible on the horizon for just a few minutes as it set between the layer of fog and the clouds.

Then we saw other lights, and in a kind of numb hope we set our course for each of them in turn. When one lasted, we tried the crucial test: 'Beacon in sight,' Néri told Cisneros, 'switch it off and on three times.' The Cisneros field switched its beacon off and on, but the hard light on which our eyes were fixed, an incorruptible star, did not flicker.

In spite of our dwindling fuel we nibbled at every golden bait, for each time it really was the beacon light, the airfield and our life, and then we had to choose another star.

We felt ourselves lost then in interplanetary space, among a hundred inaccessible planets, searching for the one true planet that was our own, the only one with landscapes we knew, houses we loved, all that we treasured.

The only one with . . . I will describe for you the image that came to me, and which may seem childish to you. But in the heart of danger a man retains his needs; I was thirsty, and I was hungry. If we did find Cisneros we would fly on after refuelling, and land at Casablanca in the cool of daybreak. Assignment completed! Néri and I would go down into town, where there are little cafés already open at dawn . . . Néri and I would find a table and sit down safely, laughing off the night, with warm croissants and milky coffee set before us. Life would give to Néri and to me that morning gift. An old peasant woman finds her God only through a painted image, or a primitive medallion, or her rosary; we too must hear a simple language if we are to hear truly. And so the joy of being alive was gathered in that aromatic and burning first taste, in that blend of milk, coffee and wheat which brings communion with peaceful pastures, with exotic plantations and with harvests, communion with all the earth. Among so many stars there was only one accessible to us, only one that could compose that fragrant breakfast bowl. But unbridgeable distances now separated our vessel and that inhabited earth. All the riches of the world were held in a speck of dust wandering amid the constellations. And the astrologer Néri sought it, praying still to the stars.

His fist suddenly thumped my shoulder, heralding a paper on which I read: 'All's well, wonderful news . . .' And my heart pounded as I waited for him to finish transcribing those few words that were to be our salvation. At last that gift from heaven reached me.

It was dated from Casablanca, which we had left the evening before. Held up in transmission, it had suddenly found us, twelve hundred miles on between clouds and fog, and lost at sea. The message was issued by the government official at Casablanca airport, and it said: 'Monsieur de Saint-Exupéry, I am obliged to advise Paris to take disciplinary action against you, for banking too close to the hangars on take-off from Casablanca.' It was true, I had banked too close to the hangars. It was also true that a man was doing his job by getting angry. In an airport office I would have received such a reproach with humility. But here it reached us where it had no right to reach us. It was out of place here among these scattered stars, this bed of fog, this threatening taste of the sea. We held our destiny in our hands with the destiny of the mail and of our vessel, we had trouble enough just steering to stay alive, and that man was purging his petty spite on us. Yet far from being annoyed, Néri and I felt a vast and sudden exultation. Here we were the masters, and he was revealing it to us. Hadn't that little corporal seen on our sleeves that we'd been promoted to the rank of captain? How dare he interrupt our dream as we patrolled solemnly between the Great Bear and Sagittarius, where the only subject on our scale and worthy of our concern was our desertion by the moon . . .

The single and immediate duty of the planet which brought forth such a man was to furnish us with precise figures for our computations among the stars. And they were wrong. For all the rest, and for the time being, the planet could just keep quiet. And Néri wrote: 'Instead of wasting time with this nonsense they'd do better to guide us somewhere . . .' By 'they' he meant all the peoples of the globe with their parliaments, their senates, their navies, their armies and their emperors. We read once more that message from a madman who claimed to have some business with us, and tacked towards Mercury.

We were saved by the strangest of chances: the hour came when, abandoning all hope of ever reaching Cisneros, and turning to fly at right angles to the coast, I decided to hold that bearing until the fuel ran out, thus preserving some hope of not coming down in the sea. Sadly, my illusory beacons had led me God knew where. Sadly, too, the thick fog through which at best we would have to dive into darkness would give us little chance of landing without disaster. But I had no choice.

The situation was so clear that I shrugged my shoulders ruefully when Néri passed me a message which, an hour earlier, would have saved us: 'Cisneros has decided to pick us up. Cisneros says 216 is doubtful . . .' Cisneros was no longer hidden in the darkness, Cisneros revealed itself at last, it was real, out there on our left. Yes, but how far away? Néri and I discussed it briefly. It was too late. We were agreed. A run for Cisneros would increase the risk of missing the coast. Néri replied: 'Only one hour's worth of fuel, therefore maintaining 93.'

The airfields, meanwhile, were waking up one by one. Into our dialogue broke the voices of Agadir, Casablanca, Dakar, all alerted by their local radio stations. The airport chiefs had alerted our comrades, who were gathering round us one by one like visitors round a sick-bed. It was a fruitless kind of warmth, but a human warmth all the same. Futile advice, but given with such affection!

And suddenly Toulouse burst in. Toulouse, airline headquarters, somewhere out there two and a half thousand miles away. Toulouse took its place without ceremony in the gathering and spoke straight to the point: 'Confirm your plane registration is F . . .' (the figures escape my memory now). We did so. 'Non-standard fuel tanks fitted. Two hours' fuel left. Head for Cisneros.'

Thus the imperatives created by a job to be done transform and enrich the world. Nor does the pilot even need such a night to discover a new meaning in familiar objects of vision. The monotonous landscape that wearies the passenger is different from the start for the crew, for whom the massing cloud on the horizon is not a backdrop: it will affect their physical being, it will challenge them with problems. They are aware of it already, measuring it, forming a bond of language with it. There is a peak ahead, still distant: what kind of face will it show? In the moonlight it will be a useful landmark. But if the pilot is flying blind, having trouble in correcting his drift and unsure of his position, that peak will change into a bomb and fill the entire night with its menace, just as a single submerged mine, drifting at the will of the current, vitiates the whole ocean.

The seas are equally fickle. To the ordinary traveller the storm remains invisible: seen from such a height, the waves have no relief and the fog patches seem immobile. But great white palm leaves seem to cover the surface, marked with veins and flaws and petrified in a kind of frost, and the seaplane crew know that this is no place to put down. For them, those palm leaves are like poisonous flowers.

And even if the journey is a pleasant one, the pilot flying along somewhere on his section of the route is not simply a witness to a scene. He is not admiring the colours of the earth and sky, the marks of the wind on the sea, the gilded clouds of twilight; they are the objects of his meditation. Just as the rustic farmer walking over his land foresees in a thousand signs the coming of spring, the danger of frost, the prospect of rain, so the professional pilot deciphers signs of snow, signs of fog, signs that the night will be a blessed one. His machine, which at first seemed to distance him from the great questions of nature, in fact subjects him even more rigorously to them. Alone within the vast tribunal that is the stormy sky, the pilot is in contention for his mailbags with three elemental divinities: mountain, sea and storm.

COMRADES

I

A group of my comrades, Mermoz among them, founded the Casablanca–Dakar route across the unconquered Sahara. Engines at that time broke down all too easily, and Mermoz was captured by the Moors after a forced landing. Uncertain whether to butcher him, they held him for two weeks and then ransomed him. And Mermoz resumed his mail flights over the same territory.

When the South American line was created, Mermoz, always the pioneer, was asked to survey the Buenos Aires–Santiago section, and to build a bridge over the Andes as he had done over the Sahara. They gave him a plane with an altitude limit of seventeen thousand feet; the highest Cordillera peaks are over twenty-two thousand. And Mermoz took off to search for the gaps. After the sand, now he confronted the mountains, those peaks that throw off their scarves of snow in the wind, that draining of the landscape's colour before a storm, those air currents swirling with such force between two rock faces that they challenge the pilot to a duel with daggers. Mermoz took on that combat with no knowledge of his opponent, nor of his chances of surviving such hand-to-hand battles. Mermoz was 'testing it' for the rest of us.

By 'testing' the Andes, he found himself at last their prisoner.

Forced down at thirteen thousand feet on a plateau with sheer sides, he and his engineer searched for two days for a way down. They were trapped. So they played their last card. They launched their plane towards the void, bouncing cruelly over the uneven ground until they dropped over the cliff edge. As it fell the plane picked up enough speed to respond to the controls. Mermoz brought its nose up as it headed for a ridge, brushed against the summit, and with water gushing out of every pipe burst by the night frost, crippled after just seven minutes in the air, he saw the Chilean plain below him like a Promised Land.

The next day he went up again.

Once the Andean exploration was complete and the flight technique perfected, Mermoz handed over that section to his comrade Guillaumet, and went on to explore the night.

Our airfields were not yet properly lit, and as Mermoz arrived in the darkness they would lay out for him the meagre guidance of three petrol flares. This held no terrors for him, and the route was opened.

When the night was tamed, Mermoz took on the Ocean. And in 1931, for the first time, the mail was carried from Toulouse to Buenos Aires in four days. On the return flight Mermoz ran out of oil over a raging sea in the middle of the South Atlantic. A ship rescued him, with the mail and his crew.

Mermoz had thus pioneered the sand and the mountains, the night and the sea. He was forced down in the desert, in the mountains, at night and at sea. And each time he came back, it was merely to set out again.

In the end, after twelve years of service, as he was flying once more over the South Atlantic, he radioed briefly that he was cutting his right rear engine. Then there was silence.

There seemed to be no great worry at that stage, but after ten minutes of silence all the radio stations from Paris to Buenos Aires began an anguished vigil. A ten-minute delay has no significance in everyday life, but in the air-mail service those minutes are heavy with meaning. At the heart of that dead time is locked a yet unknown event. Whether it be trivial or tragic, it has taken its place in history. Fate has pronounced its judgement, and there is no appeal against that judgement: an iron hand has steered a crew to a ditching in the sea that was perhaps easy, perhaps an obliteration. But those who wait have not heard that verdict.

Which of us has not experienced those ever more brittle hopes, that silence that grows more painful minute by minute like a fatal illness? We went on hoping, then the time passed and little by little the hour grew late. We had to come to terms with the truth: our comrades would never return, their resting place was that South

Atlantic whose skies they had so often furrowed. Mermoz had surely slipped away behind his work, as a harvester, after binding his sheaf with care, lies down in his field to sleep.

When a comrade dies in such a way, his death seems an act within the order of the profession, and is perhaps less wounding at first than other deaths. The pilot has certainly disappeared, he has carried out his last transfer, but his presence is not yet deeply missed as we might miss our daily bread.

For we are accustomed to long waits between our meetings. Our pilot comrades are scattered over the world, from Paris to Santiago, remote from one another like sentries who can scarcely exchange a word. Only the random chance of flight plans brings together now and then the dispersed members of this great professional family. Around a table one evening in Casablanca, Dakar or Buenos Aires, we pick up interrupted conversations after years of silence, tie the knot of old memories once more. Then we fly away again. Thus the earth is at once a desert and a store of riches. It is rich in those secret, hidden, remote gardens to which our work always brings us back some day. Life perhaps separates us from our comrades and keeps them largely from our thoughts, but they are out there somewhere, heaven knows where, silent and forgotten, but so faithful! And when our paths cross theirs, they clap their hands on our shoulders with a great surge of pleasure! Oh yes, we are accustomed to waiting . . .

But little by little we realize that we shall never again hear that pilot's bright laugh, and that the entry to that garden is forever closed to us. And then begins our true mourning; it is not heartbreaking, but just a little bitter.

Nothing, in truth, can ever replace a lost companion. Old comrades cannot be manufactured. There is nothing that can equal the treasure of so many shared memories, so many bad times endured together, so many quarrels, reconciliations, heartfelt impulses. Friendships like that cannot be reconstructed. If you plant an oak, you will hope in vain to sit soon in its shade.

For such is life. We grow rich as we plant through the early years, but then come the years when time undoes our work and cuts down our trees. One by one our comrades deprive us of their shade, and within our mourning we always feel now the secret grief of growing old.

This, then, was the moral code taught to us by Mermoz and his kind. Perhaps the greatness of a calling lies above all in the unity it creates: there is only one true form of wealth, that of human contact.

When we work merely for material gain, we build our own prison. We enclose ourselves in isolation; our coins turn to ashes and buy nothing worth living for.

If I search among my memories for those whose taste is lasting, if I write the balance sheet of the moments that truly counted, I surely find those that no fortune could have bought me. You cannot buy the friendship of a Mermoz, of a companion bound to you for ever by ordeals endured together.

No sum could buy the night flight with its hundred thousand stars, its serenity, its few hours of sovereignty.

That fresh vision of the world after a difficult phase of the flight, those trees, those flowers, those women, those smiles newly coloured with the life restored to us at dawn, that chorus of small things which are our reward . . . money cannot buy them.

Nor that night in rebel territory which is coming back to me now.

As the day was ending, three Aéropostale crews had come down on the Rio de Oro coast. Riguelle had landed first, with a broken connecting rod; Bourgat, another comrade, had landed in his turn to pick up Riguelle's crew, but some minor damage had kept him on the ground. Finally, I landed, but as I arrived night was falling. We decided to salvage Bourgat's plane, and to wait for daybreak to carry out the repair.

A year earlier our comrades Gourp and Erable, grounded at this very spot, had been butchered by rebels. We knew that a raiding party of three hundred rifles was encamped that day somewhere round Bojador. Our three very visible landings had perhaps alerted them, and we began a vigil that might well be our last.

We settled down for the night. We unloaded five or six crates of merchandise from the cargo holds, emptied them and spread them in a circle. As if it were a sentry box, we lit in each one a wretched candle, scarcely shielded from the wind. And thus, out there in the desert, in a primordial solitude on the bare husk of the planet, we built a village of men.

Gathered for the night on our village square, that patch of sand lit by the flickering light from our crates, we waited. We were waiting for the dawn that would save us, or for the Moors. And something indefinable gave that night the flavour of Christmas. We shared memories, we bantered and we sang.

We tasted the gentle excitement of a well planned celebration. And yet we were infinitely destitute. Wind, sand and stars. Austere even for a Trappist. But on that poorly lit patch, six or seven men who possessed nothing in the world but their memories were sharing invisible riches.

We had met at last. We travel side by side for years, each man enclosed in his own silence or exchanging words that convey nothing. But when the hour of danger comes we stand shoulder to shoulder. We discover that we are of the same fellowship. Our consciousness grows in the recognition of other consciousnesses. We look at one another and smile broadly. We are like the prisoner given his freedom, marvelling at the vastness of the sea.

II

Guillaumet, I shall speak a little of you as well, but I will not embarrass you with any laboured insistence on your courage and your professional merits. In narrating the finest of your exploits, there is something else that I wish to convey.

It is a quality which has no name. It might be 'seriousness', but the word is inadequate, for that quality can be accompanied by the most smiling cheerfulness. It is that essential quality of the carpenter as he addresses his piece of wood as an equal, feels it, measures it; he would never treat it carelessly, but brings all his virtues to it.

I once read a story celebrating your exploit, Guillaumet, and I have an old score to settle with that inaccurate image. You were depicted as a guttersnipe wit, as if bravery consisted in descending to schoolboy derision among the worst of dangers and in the hour of death. The writer did not know you, Guillaumet. You feel no need to deride your enemies before confronting them. In the face of

a foul storm, your judgement is: 'Here's a foul storm.' You accept it
and you take its measure.

I bring you now, Guillaumet, the testimony of my memories.

You had been missing for fifty hours, on a winter crossing of the
Andes. I came up from southern Patagonia to join Deley at Mendoza. For five long days we both searched, flying above that mass
of mountains, but found nothing. Our two machines were scarcely
adequate. It seemed to us that a hundred squadrons flying for a
hundred years would not have explored the whole of that vast
range, with its peaks rising above twenty-two thousand feet. We
had lost all hope. Even the smugglers, bandits who would commit a
crime for five francs, refused to venture into the foothills in any
rescue party: 'We'd be risking our lives up there,' they said. 'The
Andes never give up a man in winter.' Whenever Deley or I landed
at Santiago, the Chilean officials advised us similarly to suspend our
search. 'It's winter. Even if your friend survived the crash, he can't
have survived the night. When night comes to a man up there, it
turns him into ice.' And when once again I slipped between the
towering walls and pillars of the Andes, it was as if I was no longer
searching for you but keeping vigil now over your body, in the
silence of a cathedral of snow.

At last, during the second day, while I was lunching in a
Mendoza restaurant between two flights, a man pushed open the
door and shouted – oh, scarcely more than a word: 'Guillaumet's
alive!'

And all the strangers in the restaurant embraced.

Ten minutes later I had taken off with two engineers on board,
Lefebvre and Abri. Forty minutes later I had landed on a road
towards San Rafael, having somehow recognized the car which was
taking you somewhere. That was a wonderful meeting; we were all
weeping and hugging you in our arms. You were alive, resuscitated,
the author of our own miracle. It was then that you expressed, with
the first intelligible words you spoke, an admirable human pride: 'I
swear to you, no animal would have done what I have done.'

Later, you told us what had happened to you.

A storm had hurled down fifteen feet of snow in forty-eight

hours on the Chilean slopes of the Andes, choking the whole airspace and forcing the Americans of Pan-Air to turn back. Yet you took off in search of an opening in the sky. You found it a little to the south, that trap, and now at twenty thousand feet, flying over the clouds which rose to nineteen thousand and were pierced only by the highest peaks, you set your course for Argentina.

Downward currents sometimes give pilots a strange feeling of unease. The engine goes on running, but you're sinking. You pull the nose up to retain height, but the plane is losing speed and becoming limp. You loosen the reins, thinking that you have reared up too much, you let yourself drift to right or left to feel the benefit of a ridge from which the wind is rebounding favourably as from a springboard, but you go on sinking. The whole sky seems to be descending, and you feel trapped in some cosmic disaster. There is no place of safety. You try in vain to turn back to those zones where the air held you up, solid and substantial as a pillar. But there are no pillars now. Everything is disintegrating, and you are sliding down through a universal decomposition towards the snow that is rising sluggishly, coming up towards you, absorbing you.

'I'd nearly got boxed in once already,' you told us, 'but I still wasn't sure I was trapped. You come across those down-draughts above clouds that look stable, for the simple reason that at the same altitude they are endlessly changing shape. Everything is so weird in the high mountains . . .'

And what clouds!

'As soon as I was caught I let go the controls and clung to my seat so that I wouldn't be flung out. The jolting was so hard that my straps cut my shoulders and nearly snapped. The icing had cut off my artificial horizon too, and I was rolled over like a hat, from nineteen thousand down to eleven.

'At eleven thousand I caught a glimpse of a horizontal black shape that helped me to right the plane. It was a lake I knew, the Laguna Diamante. I knew it lay at the bottom of a volcanic crater; one of its sides, Maipu, is twenty-two thousand feet high. Though I was safely out of the cloud, I was still blinded by thick swirling snow, and I couldn't fly away from the lake without crashing into one of the sides of the crater. So I went on flying around the lake, about a hundred feet above it, until I ran out of fuel. After two hours on this carousel, I landed and turned over. When I freed myself from the plane, the force of the storm knocked me down. I got to my feet, and it knocked me down again. There was nothing for it but to slide in under the cabin and dig myself a shelter in the snow. I pulled some mailbags around me, and for forty-eight hours I waited.

'And then, once the storm had eased, I started to walk. I walked for five days and four nights.'

But what was left of you, Guillaumet? We had found you again, true, but you were burnt to a cinder, shrivelled, shrunken like an old woman! That very evening I took you to Mendoza, where white sheets flowed like a balm over your body. But they did not cure you. You were burdened now with that aching body, which you twisted and turned as you tried in vain to settle it in sleep. Your body could forget neither rocks nor snow. You were scarred by them. I watched your darkened, swollen face, like an overripe and bruised fruit. You were very ugly, and wretched, for you had lost the use of the beautiful tools of your trade: your hands remained numb, and when you sat on the edge of your bed to draw a breath your frozen feet hung like two dead weights. Your journey was not even over, you were still gasping for breath, and when you turned towards the pillow in search of peace, then a relentless procession of images that had been waiting impatiently in the wings was set immediately in motion under your skull. And on it went. And twenty times you took up arms against enemies reborn from their own ashes.

I filled you with herbal teas.

'Come on old fellow, drink it up!'

'You know, what really amazed me . . .'

Like a victorious boxer, but scarred by heavy blows, you were reliving your extraordinary adventure, releasing it in fragments from within you. And all through those nights of your story I could see you trudging, with no ice-axe, no rope, no food, scaling passes fifteen thousand feet high, crawling along vertical walls with bleeding hands and knees and feet in forty degrees of frost. Drained little by little of your blood, your strength and your reason, you moved on with the stubbornness of an ant, retracing your steps to go round an obstacle, picking yourself up after every fall, climbing back up slopes that led down only to the void. You allowed yourself no rest, for you would never have risen again from that bed of snow.

Every time you lost your footing, indeed, you rose instantly or you would have been turned to stone. Minute by minute the cold was petrifying you, and the price you paid for resting a moment too long after a fall was the pain in the motion of dead muscles as you struggled to your feet.

You resisted temptations. 'In the snow', you told me, 'you lose your instinct for self-preservation. After two, three or four days on your feet, all you want is sleep, and I wanted it. But I said to myself: 'If my wife believes I'm alive, she'll believe I'm on my feet. My comrades believe it too. They have faith in me. I'm a cowardly bastard if I don't keep going.'

And you kept going. Each day, with the point of your knife, you opened up your boots a little more for your freezing, swelling feet.

You confided to me this strange thing:

'From the second day onwards, you see, the hardest thing was to stop myself thinking. I was in too much pain, and my situation was just too desperate. To summon up the courage to keep going, I had to put it out of my mind. But the awful thing was that I couldn't control my mind; it went on working like a turbine. But I could still choose images for it. I would set it off on a film or a book, and the film or book would race along inside me at high speed. Then it would bring me back to my present situation. Without fail. So I would launch it out on other memories . . .'

Yet just once, after falling, stretched face down in the snow, you did not make the effort to rise. You were like a boxer suddenly drained of his passion, hearing the count sounding in another universe until it reaches ten and is beyond appeal.

'I've done my best and there's no more hope. Why go on with this torture?' All you had to do was to shut your eyes, and the world would be at peace. Rock, ice and snow, all effaced from the world. The moment those miraculous eyelids were closed, no more bruises, nor falls, nor torn muscles, nor burning ice, all that weight of life you were dragging like an ox, that weight growing heavier than a waggon. Already you could taste the cold that had become a poison, filling you like morphine with its bliss. Your life was seeking sanctuary close to your heart. Something sweet and precious nestled deep within you, as your consciousness abandoned the distant regions of your body, that beast satiated with suffering and sharing already the indifference of marble.

Even your conscience was fading away. Our cries did not reach you now; or rather, they reached you as cries in a dream. You answered happily as you walked in a dream, as your long and easy strides brought you down effortlessly to the delights of the plain. How painlessly you were gliding into a world that received you now with such affection! Guillaumet, you miser, you were making up your mind to deny us your homecoming.

Remorse came then from the very depths of your consciousness. Suddenly within the dream there were concrete details. 'I thought of my wife. My insurance policy would protect her from poverty. Yes, but the insurance company . . .'

In a case of disappearance, death certification is postponed for four years. This detail burst upon you, obliterating all the other images. There you lay, face down on a steep snow face. When the summer came, your body would come sliding down with all that slush towards one of the thousand great fissures of the Andes. You knew that. But you also knew that fifty yards ahead of you a rock was jutting out. 'I thought: if I get up, I may be able to reach it. And if I wedge my body against the stone, they'll find it when the summer comes.'

Once on your feet, you walked on for three days and two nights.

But you had no great distance in mind:

'I could tell from many signs that the end was coming. For instance, I had no choice but to stop every two hours or so, to cut my boots open a little more, to rub snow on my swelling feet, or just to rest my beating heart. But in the final days my memory was going. Each time I moved on a long way before it dawned upon me: after every stop I had forgotten something. The first time it was a glove, and that was serious in that temperature! I had put it down in front of me, and set off without picking it up. The next time it was my watch. Then my knife. Then my compass. With every stop I was becoming more destitute. 'What saves a man is to take a step. And another step. It's the same first step, repeated . . .'

*

'I swear to you, no animal would have done what I have done.' That sentence, the noblest sentence I have heard, that sentence which sets man in his rightful place, which honours him, which restores true hierarchies, kept returning to my mind. In the end sleep would eclipse your consciousness, but from that shattered, crushed, burnt body it would be born again at your waking to dominate that body. The body, then, is no more than an honest tool, no more than a servant. And that too, Guillaumet, that pride in the honest tool, you could put it into words:

'With no food, you can imagine, by the third day ... My heart wasn't going too well ... There I am, crawling along a sheer rock face, hanging over empty space, digging out holes for my fists, and suddenly my heart has engine failure. Falters, starts up again. Beating all wrong. Something in me knows that if it misses one beat too many, I'll lose my grip. Not moving an inch, I'm listening deep within myself. Never, I tell you, never in a plane have I felt so closely in touch with my engine as I felt myself suspended in those moments from my own heart. I said to it: Come on, get to work! Try to keep beating ... But it was a heart of superior stuff. It faltered, but on it went ... You can't know how proud I was of that heart!'

In that room in Mendoza where I watched over you, you would fall at last into an exhausted sleep. And I thought: If we talked to Guillaumet about his courage, he would shrug his shoulders. But to celebrate his modesty would be an equal betrayal. He is far above that mediocre virtue. If he shrugs his shoulders, it is the product of wisdom. He knows that once men are caught up in an event they have no more fear of it. Only the unknown terrifies men. Once confronted, it is no longer the unknown. Especially if it is examined with this lucid gravity. The courage of Guillaumet is above all an effect of his honesty.

But even that is not his true quality. His greatness lies in his sense of responsibility. Responsibility for himself, for his mail and for the comrades who wait in hope. In his hands he holds their grief or their joy. Responsibility for that which is being newly built, down there among the living, and in which he must play his part. Responsibility to a degree for human destiny, in as much as his work advanced it.

He is among those beings of great scope who spread their leafy branches willingly over broad horizons. To be a man is, precisely, to be responsible. It is to know shame at the sight of poverty which is not of our making. It is to be proud of a victory won by our comrades. It is to feel, as we place our stone, that we are contributing to the building of the world.

Some seek to class such men with toreadors or gamblers, and extol their contempt for death. But I don't care a damn for anyone's contempt for death. If it doesn't have its roots in an acceptance of responsibility, it is just a sign of poverty of spirit or of youthful extravagance. I once knew a young suicide. Some disappointment in love had driven him to fire a bullet carefully into his heart. I have no notion of the literary temptation to which he had succumbed as he drew on a pair of white gloves, but I remember having felt in the face of this sorry spectacle an impression not of nobility but of wretchedness. Behind that pleasant face, then, under that human skull, there had been nothing, nothing at all. Except perhaps the image of some silly girl no different from the rest.

Faced with that scrawny destiny, I remembered a real death. That of a gardener, who said to me: 'You know, I used to sweat sometimes when I was digging. My rheumatism would tug at my leg, and I used to curse my slavery. Well today, what I'd like to do is dig. Dig the earth. Digging seems so beautiful now! You're so free when you're digging! And who's going to prune my trees now?' He was leaving fallow land behind him. A planet lying fallow. He was bound by ties of love to all the soils and all the trees of the earth. He was the generous man, the man who gave unstintingly, the noble lord! He was the man of courage, like Guillaumet, battling against death in the name of his Creation.

III

THE AIRCRAFT

What does it matter, Guillaumet, if your days and nights of service are passed in the checking of gauges, in balancing your craft by gyroscope, in sounding the breath of your engines, in urging on fifteen tons of metal with your shoulders: the problems confronting you are ultimately the problems of all men, and you share the nobility of the mountain-dweller with whom you are on a direct and equal footing. Like a poet, you are a connoisseur of the first signs of dawn. From deep in the chasms of troubled nights, you have willed so often the coming of that pale flower, that gleam of light which rises from the dark lands of the east. Sometimes that miraculous spring has unfrozen slowly before your very eyes, and healed you when you thought that you were dying.

Your use of a scientific instrument has not made a dry technician of you. It seems to me that those who are alarmed by too many of our technical advances are confusing ends and means. The man who struggles in the hope of material gain alone indeed harvests nothing worth living for. But the machine is not an end in itself: it is an implement. As the plough is an implement.

If we believe that machines are ruining mankind, it may be that we are lacking a little in distance and cannot judge the effects of transformations as rapid as those that we have undergone. What are the hundred years of mechanical history when set against the two hundred thousand years of the history of man? We have scarcely begun to settle in this landscape of mines and power stations. Our life in this modern house has only just begun, and the house is not yet even complete. Everything has changed so rapidly around us: human relationships, working conditions, social customs. Our very psychology has been rocked on its most intimate foundations. The words denoting separation, absence, distance and return remain the same, but the ideas reflect a different reality. To grasp the world of today we are using a language made for the world of yesterday.

And the life of the past seems a better reflection of our nature, for the simple reason that it is a better reflection of our language.

Every step forward has removed us a little further from habits barely acquired; truly we are emigrants, still to found our homeland.

We are all young barbarians still enthralled by our new toys. What other meaning can our air races have? A man flies higher, runs faster. We forget the reason why. For the moment the race itself outweighs its purpose. And this is always so. For the colonial soldier who is founding an empire, the meaning of life is in conquest. That soldier despises the settler. But was the goal of his conquest not the establishment of that settler? In the exhilaration of our progress we have made similar use of men in the building of railways, the construction of factories, the sinking of oil wells. We have forgotten sometimes that these structures were meant to be of service to men. While we were conquering soldiers, we had the morality of soldiers. But now we must be settlers. We must bring life into this new house which as yet has no human face. If one man's truth was in building, for the other it lies in living.

No doubt our house will gradually become more human. The more perfect machines become, the more they are invisible behind their function. It seems that all man's industrial effort, all his calculations and his nights spent poring over drawings, all these visible signs have as their sole end the achievement of simplicity. It is as if only the experimentation of several generations can define the curve of a column or a ship's hull or an aeroplane fuselage, and give it the ultimate, elementary purity of the curve of a breast or a shoulder. On the surface it seems that the work of engineers, designers and research mathematicians consists only in polishing and refining, easing this joint and balancing that wing until there is no longer a wing joined visibly to a fuselage, but a perfectly developed form freed at last from its matrix, a spontaneous and mysterious whole with the unified quality of a poem. It seems that perfection is attained not when there is nothing more to add, but when there is nothing more to take away. At the climax of its evolution, the machine conceals itself entirely.

Thus the perfection of invention amounts to an absence of invention. And just as within the tool all evident mechanisms are gradually removed and we are handed an object as natural as a pebble polished by the sea, so it is equally admirable that in its very functioning the machine requires less and less awareness of its existence.

Once we were in contact with a complex workshop. Today we forget the revolving of the engine. It is at last fulfilling its function, which is to revolve just as a heart goes on beating, and we pay no attention to our heart. The tool no longer absorbs our attention. Beyond and through the tool we are rediscovering nature as it was, the nature of the gardener, the navigator, or the poet.

As he takes off, the seaplane pilot enters a relationship with water and air. When his engines are opened up and the machine is already ploughing the surface of the sea, the hull resounds like a gong as the water slaps it hard, and he feels this shuddering action in the small of his back. Moment by moment, as it gathers speed, he feels the seaplane charging itself with power. In those fifteen tons of matter he feels the coming of that maturity which makes flight possible. The pilot tightens his grip on the controls, and gradually, into his empty palms, he receives that power as a gift. Those metal organs of command become the messengers of his strength. When that maturity is reached, and with a movement more supple than the picking of a flower, the pilot separates the plane from the waters and sets it within the air.

THE PLANE AND THE PLANET

I

A plane may be just a machine, but what an analytical instrument it is! It has revealed to us the true face of the earth. Through all the centuries, in truth, the roads have deceived us. We were like the queen who desired to visit her subjects and to know if they rejoiced in her reign. Her courtiers, seeking to delude her, built pleasant stage settings along her way and paid third-rate actors to dance within them. Beyond her slender guiding thread she gained not a glimpse of her realm, and never knew that through its length and breadth she was cursed by men dying of hunger.

Just so did we make our way along our winding roads. They avoid barren lands, great rocks and sands, they are wedded to the needs of men and go from spring to spring. They guide countrymen from their barns to their wheatfields. They take up the cattle, still sleeping as they pass through the cowshed door, and deliver them in the dawn light to the alfalfa fields. They join this village to that village, for there are marriages to be made. And even if a road does venture across a desert, it twists and turns to enjoy the oases.

Deluded by curves as if by so many indulgent lies, moving on our travels past so many well watered lands, so many orchards and meadows, through all those years we embellished the image of our prison. We thought that we lived on a moist and tender planet.

But our perspective has sharpened, and we have taken a cruel step forward. Flight has brought us knowledge of the straight line. The moment we are airborne we leave behind those roads that slope gently down to water-troughs and cowsheds, or meander from town to town. Set free now from beloved servitudes, released from our dependence on natural springs, we head for our distant goals. It is only then, from high on our rectilinear course, that we discover the essential bedrock, the stratum of stone and sand and salt where life, like a patch of moss deep in hollow ruins, flowers here and there where it dares.

Thus are we changed into physicists and biologists, scrutinizing civilizations that adorn valley floors and sometimes open out miraculously like great gardens where the climate is favourable. Thus do we now assess man on a cosmic scale, observing him through our cabin windows as if through scientific instruments. Thus are we reading our history anew.

II

Just to the south of Rio Gallegos, the pilot on course for the Magellan Strait flies over an ancient lava-flow, lying seventy feet deep on the plain. Then he encounters a second, and a third, and now every rise in the ground, every seven-hundred-foot hummock has its crater within its slopes. No proud Vesuvius here: cannon mouths in the surface of the plain.

But today there is peace. It is a surprising experience in this derelict landscape, where a thousand volcanoes once answered each other with the music of their vast subterranean organs as they spat out their fire. Now you fly over a land for ever mute, adorned with black glaciers.

Further on, older volcanoes are clad already in golden turf. Sometimes there is a tree growing at the base like a plant in an old pot. Bathed in late-afternoon light and civilized by the short grass, the plain has the luxuriance of a park, and scarcely swells at all now around its giant open throats. A hare races away, a bird takes flight; life has taken possession of a new planet, its good earth laid at last over the bare star.

Finally, just before Punta Arenas, the last craters are filled. A smooth lawn clothes the contours of the volcanoes, and all is gentle now, every fissure healed and stitched by that tender flax. The land is silken, the slopes are mild. Their origin is forgotten, its dark sign effaced from the hillsides by the grass.

And here now is the southernmost town in the world, made possible by the chance presence of a little moist earth between the primeval lava and the austral ice. How powerfully the miracle of mankind is sensed here, so close to that black dross! A strange encounter! Who can know how or why man, that passing traveller, visits these gardens set out for such brief occupation: a geologic age, a day blessed among days.

I landed in the gentleness of evening. Punta Arenas! With my back against a fountain, watching the girls and so close to their grace, my sense of the human enigma is stronger still. In a world where life reaches out so readily to life, where flowers are joined with flowers in the very bed of the wind, where the swan is known to all swans, only man constructs solitude for himself.

What space is maintained between men by their spiritual nature! A girl's daydream isolates her from me; how can I share it with her? What can I know of a girl walking slowly homeward, her eyes lowered, smiling to herself, filled already with imaginative fables and charming lies? With the thoughts, the voice and the silences of a lover she has skilfully created a Kingdom; beyond its borders, for her, there are only barbarians. More so than if she were on another planet, I am aware that she is locked within her secret, within her daily actions, within the singing echoes of her memory. Born yesterday of volcanoes, of green lawns or of the brine of the sea, she is already half divine.

Punta Arenas! With my back against a fountain, I watch old women coming to draw water; of their drama I shall know nothing but these servant gestures. A child, his head against the wall behind him, is weeping silently; nothing of him will remain in my memory but a beautiful child for ever inconsolable. I am an outsider. I know nothing. I cannot enter their Empires.

How slender is the stage on which this great drama of human hatreds, friendships and joys is played out! Where do men find this taste of eternity, flung at random as they are on still-cooling lava-beds, threatened even now by the deserts of the future, threatened by the snows? Their civilizations are but fragile gildings: a volcano, a new sea, a sand storm, and they are effaced.

This town seems to be built on a true soil, deeply rich to the eye like the farmland of the Beauce. We forget that here, as elsewhere, life is a luxury, and that nowhere is the earth very deep beneath the feet of men. But I know a lake, six miles from Punta Arenas, that proves the truth. Surrounded by stunted trees and squat houses, and as humble as a farmyard pond, it is inexplicably tidal. Breathing slowly night and day among all those calm realities, those reeds, those children at play, it lives in obedience to other laws. Under its smooth surface, under the motionless ice, under that solitary crumbling boat, the energy of the moon is at work. Ocean currents are stirring in the depths of that black mass. Strange digestions are in action in that place and all the way out to the Magellan Strait, under the thin layer of grasses and flowers. Just a hundred yards wide, at the threshold of a town where men feel at home on the foundation of their earth, that lake is throbbing with the pulse of the sea.

III

We are living on a wandering planet. From time to time, thanks to the aeroplane, it reveals to us its origin: a lake connected with the moon unveils hidden kinships. I have seen other signs of this.

On the Saharan coast between Cape Juby and Cisneros, you fly at intervals over plateaux in the shape of truncated cones, varying in diameter from a few hundred yards to twenty miles. Their elevation, a thousand feet, is remarkably consistent. But in addition to this uniformity of height, they have the same colourings, the same soil texture, the same rock contours. Just as the columns of a temple emerging in isolation from the sand still show the vestiges of the crumbled architrave, so these solitary pillars bear witness to a vast plateau which once united them.

In the early years of the Casablanca–Dakar line, our equipment was fragile, and breakdowns, searches and rescues often brought landings in rebel territory. Now sand is a deceptive substance: you think it's firm, and in you sink. As for old salt-flats that look as rigid as asphalt and sound hard under your heel, they too give way sometimes under the weight of the wheels. When that happens the white salt crust cracks open and reveals a stinking black swamp. And so we would choose, when circumstances allowed, the smooth surfaces of those plateaux, where there were no hidden traps.

That security was due to a hard, heavy-textured sand, a vast accumulation of minute shells. Still intact on top of the plateau, they fragmented and cohered as you moved downwards along the ridge. In the oldest deposits, at the base of the massif, they had already become pure limestone.

Now at the time when my comrades Reine and Serre were being held by the rebels who had captured them, it came about that I put down on one of these safe havens in order to land a Moorish messenger. Before I left him, I searched with him for a way down. But in every direction our terrace ended in a vertical cliff that plunged like pleated cloth into the abyss. There was no escape.

And yet I paused a while, before taking off to seek another landing-place. I experienced a perhaps childish joy in marking with my footprints a territory unsullied until then by any man or beast. No Moor could have stormed that fortress. No European had ever explored that land. I was measuring out an infinitely virgin desert. I was the first to let that dust made of shells stream from one hand to another like a precious gold. The first to disturb that silence. On that kind of polar ice-floe, where through all eternity not a single blade of grass had formed, I was the first evidence of life, like a seed brought by the winds.

A star was already shining, and I gazed at it. That white surface, I thought, had stood open only to the stars for hundreds of thousands of years. An immaculate sheet stretched beneath the pure sky. And my heart contracted, as on the threshold of a great discovery, when I saw on that sheet, twenty yards ahead of me, a black pebble.

I was standing on shells to a depth of a thousand feet. The vast structure, in its entirety, was in itself an absolute ruling against the presence of any stone. Flints might be sleeping deep down within it, born of the planet's slow digestive processes, but what miracle could have brought one of them to this all-too-new surface? My heart pounded as I picked up my discovery: a hard, black pebble the size of a fist, heavy like metal, cast in the shape of a teardrop.

A sheet stretched beneath an apple tree can gather only apples, a sheet stretched beneath the stars can gather only star-dust: never had any aerolite given such clear proof of its origin.

And very naturally, as I lifted my head, the thought came to me that from that celestial apple tree other fruits must have fallen. I would find them exactly at the point of their fall, since for hundreds of thousands of years nothing could have disturbed them, and since they would not merge with other materials. I set off at once on an exploration, to test my hypothesis.

It was proven. I collected my discoveries at a rate of about one per hectare. Each one with that appearance of moulded lava. Each with that black, diamond hardness. And thus did I witness, in a compelling compression of time high up there on my starry rain-gauge, that slow and fiery downpour.

IV

But the most wondrous thing was that there on the planet's curved back, between that magnetic sheet and those stars, stood a human consciousness in which that rain could find reflection as in a mirror. On a pure mineral stratum, a dream is a miracle. And I remember a waking dream . . .

Forced down once more in a landscape of deep sand, I was waiting for the dawn. The golden hills offered up their luminous slopes to the moon, and others rose up in the shadow to its frontier with the light. In this deserted factory of darkness and moonlight there reigned the peace of work in abeyance and the silence of a trap, and I fell asleep within it.

When I awoke I saw nothing but the pool of the night sky, for I was lying on a ridge with my arms stretched out, facing that hatchery of stars. With no understanding at that moment of those depths, I was seized by vertigo, for with no root to cling to, no roof or tree branch between those depths and me, I was already adrift and sinking, abandoned to my fall like a diver.

But I did not fall. I found myself bound to the earth, from nape to heel. I let it take my weight, and felt a kind of appeasement. Gravity seemed as sovereign as love.

I felt the earth propping up my back, sustaining me, lifting me, carrying me within nocturnal space. I found myself adhering to the planet, held by a force like the force that pins you to a waggon on a curve, and I found joy in this excellent rampart, this solidity, this security, as I sensed beneath my body the curved deck of my ship.

So strongly was I aware of being in motion that I would have heard without astonishment, rising from deep within the earth, the complaint of matter shifting under stress, the groan of the old sailing ship as it heels, the sustained and bitter moan of the mishandled barge. But within the density of the earth the silence endured. Yet the force was manifest in my shoulders, harmonious, sustained, changeless for eternity. As the lead-weighted bodies of dead galley-slaves inhabit the bottom of the sea, so was this a homeland for me.

And I reflected on my condition, lost in the desert and in danger, naked between sand and stars, distanced from the poles of my life by an excess of silence. For I knew that to rejoin them I would consume days, weeks, months if no plane found me, and if the Moors did not slaughter me tomorrow. Here, I had nothing left in the world. I was nothing but a mortal being lost between sand and stars, conscious only of the sweetness of drawing breath . . .

And yet I found that I was filled with dreams.

They came to me soundlessly like the waters of a spring, and at first I did not understand the gentle joy that was flowing into me. There was neither voice nor image, but the awareness of a presence, a friendship that was very close and already half known by intuition. Then I understood, closed my eyes, and surrendered myself to the enchantment of my memory.

There was a park, somewhere, heavy with dark fir trees and linden, and an old house that I loved. It mattered little whether it was near or far, that it could neither warm me in my flesh nor shelter me, confined as it was to its role in my dream: its existence was sufficient to fill my night with its presence. I was no longer a body washed up on a shore; I was finding my way within it, I was the child of that house, filled with the memory of its smells, filled with the coolness of its hallways, filled with the voices that had given it life. There was even the song of the frogs in the pools; they came to be with me here. I needed those thousand points of reference to recognize myself, to discover what absences composed the taste of this desert, to find a meaning in this silence formed of a thousand silences, where even the frogs were mute.

No, I was no longer on the edge between sand and stars. The

setting now gave me only a cold message. And that very taste of eternity which I seemed to have received from it now revealed to me its origin. I saw once more the great solemn cupboards of the house, half open to show piles of sheets as white as snow, half open on stores frozen with snow. The old housekeeper trotted like a rat from one to the other, always checking, unfolding, folding, counting once more the bleached linen, crying out: 'Oh, Lord above, how dreadful,' at every sign of wear that was a threat to the eternity of the house, then rushing away to scorch her eyes under some lamp, repairing the weft of those altar-cloths, mending those sails for three-masters, serving something unknown and greater than herself: a God, or a ship.

Yes, I owe you a page, Mademoiselle. When I came home from my first journeys, I found you with your needle in your hand, drowned to the knees in your white surplices, each year a little more wrinkled, a little greyer, still preparing those uncreased sheets for our slumbers, those seamless cloths for our dinners, those festivals of crystal and light. I would go to see you in your linen-room, sit down facing you and tell you about my deadly dangers to disturb your calm, to open your eyes to the world, to corrupt you. You used to say that I had scarcely changed. Even as a child I made holes in my shirts – oh, how dreadful! – and took the skin off my knees; then I came home to be patched up, like this evening. No, Mademoiselle, no, I was back not from the other end of the park but from the other end of the world, and I brought with me the acrid smell of desert places, the whirling sandstorm, the vivid tropical moonlight! Yes, yes, you said, boys race about and break their bones, and think they're big and strong. No, Mademoiselle, no, I've seen beyond our park! If only you knew how insignificant these leafy shadows are! How lost they seem among the sands, the granite rocks, the virgin forests and the swamplands of the earth. Do you even know that there are lands where men instantly raise their rifles on meeting you? That there are deserts where men sleep in the ice-cold night with no roof, Mademoiselle, no bed, no sheets . . .

'Oh, you barbarian!' you would say.

I could no more shake her faith than that of an altar-server in a church. And I pitied her humble destiny, for it made her blind and deaf . . .

But that night, in the Sahara, naked between sand and stars, I rendered justice to her.

I do not know what is taking place within me. This weight unites me with the ground while so many stars are magnetized. Another weight restores me to myself. I feel my weight drawing me in so many directions! My dreams are more real than these dunes, this moon, these presences. Ah! the miracle of a house is not that it shelters or warms you, nor that its walls belong to you. But that it has slowly deposited in us all those stored resources of gentle joy. And that deep within the heart it forms the shadowy range of hills in which our dreams, like spring waters, are born . . .

Sahara, my Sahara, you are entirely bewitched by an old woman at her spindle!

V

OASIS

I have already spoken so much of the desert that before saying more about it I would like to describe an oasis. The one whose image comes back to me is not lost deep in the Sahara. But another miracle of the aeroplane is that it plunges you straight into the heart of an enigma. You were the biologist studying the human anthill through your porthole, you were contemplating dryly the towns fixed on their plain, at the centre of the radiating roads which nourish them like arteries with the juice of the fields. But a needle has quivered on a gauge, and that green clump down there has become a universe. You are the prisoner of a patch of grass in a sleeping park.

Distance is not the measure of remoteness. The wall of our own garden may enclose more secrets than the Wall of China, and the soul of a little girl is more fully guarded by silence than are the Saharan oases by the density of the sands.

I will tell of a brief stop I made somewhere in the world. I put down near Concordia, in the Argentine, but it could have been anywhere at all, so universal is the mystery.

I had landed in a field, with no idea that I was about to live through a fairy-tale. There was nothing special about the Ford in which I was being driven, nor the quiet couple who had gathered me up.

'We'll give you a bed for the night . . .'

But at a bend in the road a clump of trees came into view in the moonlight, and behind the trees was the house. A strange house! Squat, massive, almost a fortress. A castle of legend, offering within its portal a shelter that was as peaceful, as secure, as protected as a monastery.

Then two girls appeared. They looked me gravely up and down, like two judges posted on the threshold of a forbidden kingdom; the younger one pouted and tapped the ground with a green stick, then, with the introductions done, they each held out a hand to me without a word but with a strangely challenging air, and disappeared.

I was amused, and I was charmed. It had all been as simple, silent and stealthy as the first word of a secret.

'Not very sociable,' the father said simply, and we went inside.

I used to love that ironic grass in Paraguay, pushing its nose up between the cobblestones of the capital to see, on behalf of the invisible yet always present virgin forest, whether men still hold the city, whether perhaps the hour has come to shove all these stones aside. I loved that form of dilapidation which expresses merely an excess of wealth. But here I was overcome with wonder.

Here everything was dilapidated, but most attractively so, in the way of an old tree covered in moss, its surface cracked by time like a wooden bench where lovers have been sitting together for ten generations. All the panelling was decayed, the doors were pitted, the chairs were rickety. But if nothing here was repaired, it was polished with a passion. Everything was clean, waxed and gleaming.

This gave the drawing-room an extraordinary intensity, like the face of a wrinkled old woman. I was in awe of it all, of the cracked walls, the torn ceilings, and above all the wooden floor; it caved in here, wobbled there, but everywhere it was polished, varnished, glossy. This bizarre house suggested no neglect, no casualness, but a remarkable reverence. No doubt each passing year added something to its charm, to the complexity of its face and the intensity of its welcoming atmosphere, as well as to the risks run in journeying from the drawing-room to the dining-room.

'Take care!'

There was a hole, and I was warned that in such a hole I could easily have broken my leg. No one was responsible for that hole: it was the work of time. This sovereign contempt for apologies had something very lordly about it. No one said: 'We could fill in these holes, we're rich, but . . .' Nor was I told – though it was the truth – 'We've leased it from the town council for thirty years. Repairs are their responsibility. Everybody's being stubborn . . .' They disdained explanations, and such relaxation charmed me.

'It's a bit run-down . . .' was the most that was said. But it was said with such lightness of tone that I suspected my friends were not too distressed about it. Could you see a crew of builders, carpenters, cabinet-makers and plasterers spreading their sacrilegious implements through such a past, and reshaping for you within a week an unrecognizable house where you would think yourself a visitor? A house without mystery, without secret corners, without traps underfoot, without oubliettes – in other words, a municipal reception suite.

The disappearance of the two girls in that conjuror's house was quite natural. What must the attics be, when the drawing-room contained the riches of an attic! And when you could already sense that from the smallest half-open cupboard would tumble bundles of yellowed letters, great-grandfather's receipts, more keys than there are locks in the house and of course not one to fit any existing keyhole. Wonderfully pointless keys that confound reason and bring dreams of underground chambers, buried caskets, golden louis.

'Shall we go in to dinner?'

We went in to dinner. As we passed from room to room I inhaled that old library smell, hanging in the air like incense and worth all the perfumes of the world. And above all I liked the carrying of the lamps. Real, heavy lamps, moved by hand from room to room as in my earliest childhood days, stirring marvellous shadows on the walls. Bouquets of light and black palm leaves moved with them. Then, when the lamps were finally set down, the shores of light grew still, as did the vast reserves of darkness all around, in which the woodwork went on creaking.

The two girls reappeared as mysteriously and as silently as they had vanished. Gravely they took their places at table. No doubt they had fed their dogs and their birds, opened their windows on to the clear night and tasted in the evening wind the smell of the plants. Now, unfolding their napkins, they were watching me out of the corner of their eye, cautiously, wondering if they would be finding me a place among their pets. For they also had an iguana, a mongoose, a fox, a monkey and a hive of bees, all living on top of each other in marvellous understanding and forming a new earthly paradise. The girls reigned over all the animals in creation, charming them with their little hands, feeding and watering them, and telling them tales to which, from the mongoose to the bees, all listened.

I fully expected to see two such lively young girls employing all their critical faculties and all their subtlety in passing a rapid, secret and definitive judgement on the male sitting opposite them. In my own childhood, my sisters gave marks to guests who were honouring our table for the first time. And when conversation lapsed, a cry of 'eleven!' would ring out in the silence, and only my sisters and I would appreciate its charm.

I was a little worried by my experience of this game, and even more troubled to sense how knowing my judges were. They were judges who could tell cheating animals from artless animals, who could tell from their fox's walk whether he was in an approachable mood, and who possessed such a deep awareness of the movements of instinct.

I liked those sharp eyes and those honest souls, but I really wished they would play some other game. Yet in base fear of their 'eleven' I passed them the salt and poured them some wine, but when I looked up again I found the mild gravity of judges who were not to be bought.

Flattery itself would have been useless: they knew no vanity. No vanity, but they did have a fine pride, and thought better of themselves without my help than anything I might have dared to say. I did not even think of cultivating any prestige from my profession, for it is equally audacious to climb to the topmost branches of a plane tree, simply to see whether the brood of little birds are growing their feathers as they should, and to greet one's friends.

And my two silent fairies went on watching me as I ate, with my eyes meeting their furtive glances so often that I said no more. In the silence that followed something hissed gently on the wooden floor, rustled beneath the table, then was silent. I looked up in curiosity. And then, no doubt satisfied with her examination but using her final touchstone, and sinking her uncivilized young teeth into her bread, the younger one explained to me in all simplicity, and with a candour with which she hoped to astound the barbarian, if that was what I was:

'Those were the vipers.'

Content now, she said no more, as if that explanation should have been enough for anyone other than a complete fool. Her sister shot a glance in my direction to assess my first reaction, and both then gazed towards their plates with the sweetest and most ingenuous expression in the world.

'Ah . . . The vipers . . .'

Naturally those words slipped out. That slithering around my legs, that brushing against my calves . . . vipers.

Fortunately for me, I smiled. Without forcing it: they would have sensed that. I smiled because I felt joyful, because this house, decidedly, pleased me more with every passing minute; and because I felt the desire to know more about the vipers. The elder girl came to my aid:

'They nest in a hole under the table.'

'They come home about ten in the evening,' her sister added. 'They hunt in the daytime.'

Now, in my turn, I looked surreptitiously at those girls. That subtlety, that silent laughter behind the placid faces. And I admired the royal authority they exercised . . .

I am dreaming, today. All that is very far away. What has become of those two fairies? Married, probably. But will that have changed them? The passage from girlhood to womanhood is such a serious thing. What do they do in their new homes? What has happened to their relationship with wild grasses and with snakes? They were in touch with something universal. But the day comes when the woman awakes within the girl, with the dream of awarding a 'nineteen' at last. That nineteen is a burden on the heart. Then some fool presents himself. For the first time those sharp eyes deceive themselves, and light him in beautiful colours. If the fool speaks in verse, he is taken for a poet. Surely he understands the pitted floor, surely he loves mongooses, surely he is gratified by the intimacy of the viper swaying around his legs beneath the table. He receives a heart which is a wild garden, he who loves only trim parklands. And the fool takes the princess away into slavery.

VI

IN THE DESERT

I

Such sweet pleasures were forbidden to us when, as airline pilots, we were prisoners of the Saharan sands for days, or weeks, or years, steering our course from one small fort to another, with no return home. That desert offered no such oasis: gardens and young girls – what myths! Far away, of course, where we might live again once our work was done, a thousand girls were waiting for us. There, of course, among their mongooses or their books, they were patiently forming their own exquisite souls. And of course, they were growing in beauty . . .

But I know solitude. Three years in the desert have taught me its taste. What is frightening is not the consuming of youth out there in that mineral landscape, but the perception that far away from you the whole world is growing old. The trees have formed their fruit, the earth has brought forth its wheat, the women are already lovely. The season is moving on, you want to hurry home . . . The season is moving on, and you are trapped far away . . . And the good things of the earth are slipping between your fingers like the fine sand of the dunes.

In normal life men do not experience the passage of time. They live in a provisional stillness. But we experienced it with each port of call reached, feeling the force of the ever-moving trade winds. We were like the traveller on the express train, filled with the sound of the axles pounding in the darkness; from the clusters of light streaming wastefully away behind the glass he can guess only dimly at the flow of the country, its villages, its enchanted domains of which he can grasp nothing, for he is a traveller. Alive with a slight fever, our ears whistling still with the noise of the flight, we too felt that we were in motion, despite the stillness of our airfield. We discovered that we too were being carried along towards an unknown future, through the thoughts of the winds and by the pulsing of our hearts.

Rebel tribesmen amplified the desert. Nights at Cape Juby were interrupted every quarter of an hour as if by the chiming of a clock: each sentry signalled to the next with a loud regulation call. That is how the Spanish fort at Cape Juby, far out in rebel territory, protected itself against a threat that never showed its face. And we, the passengers on this eyeless ship, listened to the call growing louder as it passed from man to man, describing above us the trajectories of seabirds.

And yet we loved the desert.

If at ᶜrst it is merely emptiness and silence, that is because it does not open itself to transient lovers. Even a simple village in our own country conceals itself. If we do not renounce the rest of the world in its favour, if we do not enter into its traditions, its customs and its rivalries, we remain blind to the homeland it is for some. This is even truer of the man immured in his cloister a stone's throw from us, living by rules unknown to us; he stands in a truly Tibetan isolation, in a distant place where no plane will ever set us down. To what purpose would we visit his cell? It is empty. The empire of man is within man. And thus the desert is not composed of sand, nor of Tuaregs, nor even of Moors armed with rifles . . .

But on this day we have experienced thirst. And we discover for the first time today that our familiar well radiates its influence over the whole vast expanse, as an unseen woman casts a spell over an entire house. A well spreads its power far and wide, like love.

At first the sands are empty, then comes the day when, fearing the approach of a raiding party, we read within their contours the folds of the great cloaks in which the raiders are wrapped. Thus those raiders transfigure the sands.

We have accepted the rules of the game, and the game now forms us in its own image. It is within us that the Sahara reveals itself. To approach it is not to visit an oasis, it is to make our religion of a spring.

II

On my very first flight I knew the taste of the desert. Riguelle, Guillaumet and I had been forced down near the Nouatchott fort. That little Mauritanian outpost was as remote then from all other life as an island in the open sea. An old sergeant was shut away there with his fifteen Senegalese. He welcomed us as if we had been sent from heaven:

'Oh, it does me good to talk to you . . . Oh, it does me good!'

It was doing him good: he was weeping.

'You're the first in six months. I get reprovisioned every six months. Sometimes it's the lieutenant, sometimes it's the captain. Last time it was the captain . . .'

We were still feeling bewildered. Two hours from Dakar, where our lunch is being prepared, and the connecting rods break up, changing our destiny. And now we're playing the role of apparitions for an old sergeant in tears.

'Come on, have a drink, it's such a pleasure for me to offer you some wine! Just think! When the captain came, I had none left to give the captain.'

I have used this story in a novel, but it wasn't fiction. He told us:

'Last time, there wasn't even enough left to drink his health . . . And I was so ashamed, I asked to be relieved.'

To drink his health! To clink glasses with another man who has just leapt down from a dromedary's back, dripping in sweat! To live for six months in expectation of that moment. Polishing weapons for the month before it, furbishing the outpost from bunker to attic. Then sensing the approach of the blessed day itself, scanning the horizon with unwearying eyes to detect that cloud of dust in which the Atar Camel Corps, when it comes, will be enveloped . . .

But there is no wine: there can be no celebration. No toasts. Dishonour laid bare . . .

'I hope he'll come back soon. I'm waiting for him . . .'

'Where is he, sergeant?'

And the sergeant replied, gesturing towards the sands:

'Who knows? He's everywhere, that captain!'

*

That night on the fortress terrace was real too; we talked about the stars. There was nothing else to watch. They were there in their fullness, as seen from a plane, but holding steady.

In a plane you let yourself go when the night is too beautiful, you are scarcely flying it at all, and gradually the plane tilts to the left. You think you are horizontal, and there under your right wing is a village. There are no villages in the desert. A fishing fleet at sea, then. But in the vast Sahara there are no fishing fleets. Well, what then? You smile at your mistake, and you gently straighten up the plane. The village is back in its place. You hook back on to the panoply the constellation you had let slip. Village? Yes, a village of stars. But from high up on the fortress roof there is just a desert that seems frozen, just motionless waves of sand. Firmly attached constellations. And the sergeant has some words to say about them:

'Hey, I know which way is which . . . Steer by that star, it'll take you straight to Tunis!'

'Are you from Tunis?'

'No. My cousin. She is.'

A long silence follows. But the sergeant cannot hold anything back from us:

'One of these days, I'll go to Tunis.'

Surely by another route than heading for that star. Unless one day, on expedition, a dried-up well delivers him up to the poetry of delirium. Then the star, the cousin and Tunis will merge into one, and he will set out on that inspired march which is imagined by the uninitiated to be a torment.

'I once asked the captain for leave to go to Tunis, with my cousin in mind. And he answered . . .'

'What was his answer?'

'He answered: "The world's full of cousins." And as it wasn't so far, he sent me to Dakar.'

'Was your cousin pretty?'

'The one in Tunis? Yes, of course. She had blonde hair.'

'No, the one in Dakar.'

Sergeant, we could have embraced you for your frustrated, melancholy answer:

'She was a Negress . . .'

*

What was the desert for you, sergeant? It was a God for ever on the march towards you. And the sweetness of a blonde cousin beyond three thousand miles of sand.

And the desert for us? It was what was being born within us. What we were learning about ourselves. We too, that night, were in love with a cousin and a captain . . .

III

Port-Étienne, on the edge of the unconquered territories, could not be called a town. There is a fort, a hangar, and a wooden hut for our crews. Surrounded by absolute desert, it is practically invincible in spite of its feeble military resources. To attack it, any raiders would have to cross such a belt of sand and fire that they would exhaust their strength and their water supplies. Yet in living memory there has always been, somewhere up north, a razzia marching on Port-Étienne. Each time the captain-governor comes to take tea with us he shows us its route on the map, as if he were recounting the legend of a beautiful princess. But that razzia never arrives; the sand dries it up each time like a river. We call them the phantom raiders. The nightly government allocation of grenades and cartridges remains sleeping in its box at the foot of our beds. And there is no enemy to fight but silence, in the destitution that is our chief protection. And Lucas, the airfield manager, winds his gramophone night and day; so remote from life, it speaks to us in a half-forgotten language, awakening an undefined melancholy which is strangely like thirst.

We dined at the fort tonight, and the captain-governor displayed his garden to us. He has indeed received from France three crates of genuine earth. It has travelled two and half thousand miles, and within it three green leaves are growing; we stroke them as if they were jewels. The captain says of them: 'This is my garden.' And when the all-desiccating sandstorms blow, the garden is taken down to the cellar.

Our quarters are half a mile from the fort, and we are walking back from dinner, in the moonlight. The sand is pink beneath the moon. We can sense our destitution, but the sand is pink. Then a sentry's call re-establishes pathos in the world. The whole Sahara is afraid of our shadows and is asking us for the password, because there are raiders on the march.

All the voices of the desert are reverberating in that sentry's cry. The desert is not an empty house: a Moorish caravan is magnetizing the darkness.

We might believe ourselves secure. And yet sickness, accidents, raiders, so many dangers are roaming! Man is an earthly target for secret marksmen. The Senegalese sentry, like a prophet, is there to remind us of it.

'Frenchmen!' we reply. We pass before the black angel, and breathe more easily. Oh, how that sense of danger has ennobled us ... though it was so far away, so lacking in urgency, so cushioned by the sand: but the world is different now. The desert is superb once more. Somewhere on the march there are raiders who will never reach their goal; they give it its divinity.

It's eleven o'clock now. Lucas comes back from the radio-room and tells me the Dakar plane is due at midnight. All's well on board. By ten past midnight the mail will be transferred to my aircraft, and I will take off for the North. I shave carefully in a chipped mirror. From time to time, with a towel round my neck, I go to the door and gaze at the naked sand: the night is fine, but the wind is dropping. Back at the mirror, I am thoughtful: sometimes the dropping of a wind that has blown for months can disturb the whole sky. Now I am climbing into my harness: safety lamps tied to my belt, altimeter, pencils. I go to see Néri, who will be my radio operator on this flight. He too is shaving. 'Everything all right?' I ask him. For the moment everything is all right. These preparations are the easiest stage of the flight. But I hear a crackling sound: a dragonfly has flown into my lamp. I cannot say why, but I feel a contraction in my heart.

Outside again, I gaze around: all is clear. A rock face on the edge of the airfield stands out against the sky as if it were daylight. Over the desert, as in a well-kept house, a great silence reigns. But now a green moth and then two dragonflies strike my lamp. And once more I feel within me a muted emotion, perhaps joy, perhaps fear; it is something very deep, very obscure, scarcely formed. From far away someone is speaking to me. Is it intuition? I go out once more: the wind has died down entirely. The air is still cool. But I have received a warning. I can guess, I believe I can guess what I am waiting for: am I right? Neither the sky nor the sand have given me any sign, but two dragonflies have spoken to me, and a green moth.

I climb a dune and sit, facing east. If I am right, 'it' won't be long in coming. What else could these dragonflies be doing here, hundreds of miles from the inland oases? Small pieces of wreckage washed up on the beaches are evidence of a cyclone raging at sea. In the same way these insects tell me that a sandstorm is in motion; coming from the East, it has laid waste the distant palm groves and stripped them of their green moths. I have already felt its spray. And solemnly because it is a confirmation, and solemnly because it is heavy with menace, and solemnly because there is a storm within it, the East wind is rising now. Its fragile breath barely touches me. I am the farthest shore lapped by the wave. Twenty yards back from me, no canvas would stir. Its burning sigh has wound around me just once, in a caress that seemed lifeless. But I know for certain that the Sahara is drawing in its breath and will send forth a second sigh. And that within three minutes the wind-sock on our hangar will be ruffled. Within ten minutes the sky will be filled with sand. We will be taking off soon into that blaze, that backfire of desert flame.

But that is not what stirs my emotions. What fills me with a barbarian joy is that I have grasped a secret and unspoken language, I have scented a trail like a primitive tribesman within whom all the future is foretold by such slight murmurings, and I have read that anger in the wingbeats of a dragonfly.

IV

Out there we were in contact with the unconquered Moorish tribes. They emerged from deep within those forbidden territories over which we flew, ventured as far as the forts at Cape Juby or Cisneros to buy sugar loaves or tea, then disappeared once more within their mystery. At each contact we would try to tame a few of them.

When influential chiefs turned up, we would take them on board (with the management's approval) and show them the world. The purpose was to break down their arrogance, for it was through contempt rather than hatred that they butchered their prisoners. If they met us on the outskirts of a fortress, they did not bother to insult us; they merely turned away and spat. This arrogance was born of an illusion of power. Many a time I heard these words from one of those leaders of three hundred battle-ready riflemen: 'You Frenchmen are fortunate that your country is more than a hundred days' march from here . . .'

So we took them flying, and three of them even visited that unknown France. They were of the same race as those who once came to Senegal with me, and who wept at the sight of trees.

When I met them again in their tents, they were singing the praises of the music-halls where naked women danced among the flowers. These were men who had never seen a tree or a spring or a rose, who knew only from the Koran of the existence of gardens with flowing streams, for thus it describes paradise. For them that paradise and its beautiful captives could be reached only through a bitter death in the sand from an infidel's rifle shot, after thirty years of wretchedness. But God has deceived them, for He grants to the French all these treasures and yet exacts from them in return no payment by thirst or by death. That is why those old chiefs are so reflective now, why they drop their defences as they consider the empty Sahara that stretches around their tents, and confide:

'You know . . . the God of the French is more generous to the French than the God of the Moors is to the Moors!'

A few weeks earlier they were being shown the French Alps. Their guide had led them to a powerful waterfall, a kind of braided column filled with sound:

'Taste it,' he had said.

It was sweet water. Water! How many days' march does it take here to reach the nearest well, and even if you find it how many hours to dig out the sand and reach a muddy liquid mixed with camel urine? Water! At Cape Juby, Cisneros and Port-Étienne, the

Moorish children with empty tins in their hands ask not for money, but for water:

'Give me a little water, give . . .'

'If you're good.'

Water is worth its weight in gold; the smallest drop kindles in the sand the green spark of a blade of grass. If rain falls anywhere, a great exodus brings life to the Sahara. The tribes ride towards the grass that will grow two hundred miles away . . . And that miserly water, of which not a drop has fallen at Port-Étienne for ten years, came roaring down in the Alps as if the world's supply were pouring forth from a punctured reservoir.

'It's time to leave,' said the guide. But they would not move.

'Let us stay a little longer . . .'

They stood in silence, grave and speechless before that enactment of a solemn mystery. What was cascading from the womb of the mountain was life itself, the very blood of men. One second's flow would have revived whole caravans, demented with thirst and sunk for ever in the infinity of salt lakes and mirages. Here God was made manifest: you could not turn your back on Him. God had opened the flood-gates and was showing his power: the three Moors stood motionless.

'There's no more to see. Come . . .'

'We must wait.'

'Wait for what?'

'The end.'

They wanted to wait until the moment when God would grow weary of his extravagant folly, for He is quick to repent, and He is miserly.

'But this water has been flowing for a thousand years! . . .'

And so they do not dwell now, as we talk tonight, on the waterfall. It is better to keep silent on certain miracles. Better still not to think too much about them, or all understanding will crumble, and even God will be doubted . . .

'The God of the French, you see . . .'

But how well I know those barbarian friends of mine. There they sit, troubled in their faith, disconcerted, and so near now to submission. They dream of being supplied with barley by French quartermasters, and given guaranteed security by our Saharan brigades. And it is true that when they are subjugated there will be material gains for them.

But all three are of the blood of El Mammun, the Emir of the Trarza peoples (if I have his name correctly). I knew him when he was our vassal. Granted official honours for services rendered, enriched by the administration and respected by the tribes, it seemed that he lacked nothing in visible wealth. But one night, with no warning sign, he butchered the officers he was escorting into the desert, seized camels and guns, and rejoined the unconquered tribes.

Treason is the name given to such a sudden revolt and flight, at once heroic and desperate, on the part of a chief who is then forever outlawed in the desert; a brief rocket-burst of glory that will soon be snuffed out on the Atar Camel Corps' defences. And such accesses of madness provoke astonishment.

Yet the story of El Mammun was that of many other Arabs. He was growing old, and ageing brings meditation. So it was that he realized one night that he had betrayed the God of Islam, and had sullied his hand by sealing in a Christian hand a pact in which all the losses were his.

And indeed, what were barley and peace to him? As a warrior stripped of rank and turned into a shepherd, suddenly he remembers that he once lived in a Sahara where every fold in the sand was rich in hidden menace, where out in the darkness the encampment had look-outs at all its furthest points, where news of enemy movements made hearts beat faster around the night fires. He remembers a taste of the high seas which is never forgotten once a man has savoured it.

He is a wanderer stripped of glory now, in a pacified vastness stripped of all splendour. Only now has the Sahara become a desert.

Perhaps he revered the officers he will murder. But the love of Allah takes precedence.

'Good night, El Mammun.'

'May God protect you!'

The officers wrap their blankets around them and stretch out on the sand with their faces turned to the stars, as if they are on a raft. All the stars are there, revolving slowly, a whole sky marking the hour. The moon is there, dipping towards the sands, descending towards nothingness through His Wisdom. Soon the Christians will fall asleep. A few minutes more and only the stars will shine. And then, for the degenerate tribes to be restored to their past splendour, for there to be once more those glorious charges which alone bring radiance to the sands, the feeble cry of these Christians will be sufficient as they are drowned in their sleep . . .

And the handsome sleeping lieutenants are slaughtered.

V

Today at Juby, Kemal and his brother Mouyan have invited me to their tent, and I am drinking tea. Mouyan is staring at me in silence, maintaining an uncivil taciturnity with his blue veil pulled across his mouth. Only Kemal speaks to me and does the honours:

'My tent, my camels, my wives, my slaves are yours.'

Mouyan, his eyes still fixed on me, leans towards his brother and speaks a few words, then returns to his silence.

'What is he saying?'

'He says that Bonnafous has stolen a thousand camels from the tribes of R' Guibat.'

I have not met this Captain Bonnafous, an officer in the Atar Camel Corps, but I know from the Moors that he is a legend among them. They speak of him with anger, but as a kind of god. The sand appreciates in value by his presence. No one knows how, but he has appeared again this very day at the rear of the southward-marching razzias, stealing their camels by the hundred, forcing them to turn back and fight him to save the treasures they thought were safe. And now, having saved Atar by this archangelic apparition, and having set up his camp on a high limestone plateau, he stands there tall and upright like a victory token to be seized, and his magnetism is such that the tribes must march towards his sword.

Looking harder at me now, Mouyan speaks again.

'What is he saying?'

'He says we will leave tomorrow to strike against Bonnafous. Three hundred riflemen.'

I knew something was up. Camels being led to the wells for the past three days, endless discussions, a vibrant excitement. As if an invisible sailing ship were being rigged out, with the sea wind that will carry her away already in the air. Bonnafous will turn every southward step into a step rich in honour. I can no longer distinguish what is hate and what is love in such departures.

It is a magnificent thing to have such a fine enemy to kill. Wherever he appears, the tribes nearby fold their tents, gather their camels and flee in fear of meeting him face to face, but the more distant tribes spin into a dizzy fever like that of love. Men tear themselves away from the peace of their tents, from the embrace of their women, from the contentment of sleep. They discover that nothing in the world, after two months of exhausting southward travel, of burning thirst and long waits crouching under sandstorms, could equal the joy of coming unexpectedly at dawn upon the Atar Camel Corps and – God willing – of killing Captain Bonnafous.

'Bonnafous is a great man,' Kemal acknowledges.

Now I know their secret. As men who desire a woman dream of her indifferent passing footsteps and turn and turn again all through the night, wounded, scorched by her indifferent passing steps in their dream, the distant steps of Bonnafous torment them. Outflanking the raiders sent against him, this Christian in Moorish clothing who leads two hundred Moorish buccaneers has entered rebel territory, where the humblest of his own men could awake one day free from French constraints, free from servitude, and with impunity sacrifice him to his God on those stone tables. Once out there nothing but his prestige controls them, and his very weakness terrifies them. And tonight he moves indifferently to and fro amid their noisy sleep, and his footsteps ring in the very heart of the desert.

Mouyan is deep in thought, still motionless at the back of the tent, like a bas-relief carved in blue granite. His eyes alone are shining, and his silver dagger that has ceased to be a plaything. How he has changed since he called together the raiding party! He is aware as never before of his own nobility, and crushes me with his contempt; for he is to ride against Bonnafous, he is to move off at dawn, driven by a hatred that bears all the signs of love.

Yet again he leans towards his brother, whispers something, and looks at me.

'What is he saying?'

'He says he will shoot you if he meets you away from the fort.'

'Why?'

'He says you have aeroplanes, you have the wireless and you have Bonnafous, but you do not have the truth.'

I am being judged by Mouyan, sitting motionless in his blue veils and his sculptured folds:

'He says you eat green salad like the goats and pork like the pigs. Your shameless women show their faces: he has seen them. He says you never pray. He says: what good to you are your planes, your wireless and your Bonnafous, if you do not have the truth?'

And I admire this Moor who is about to defend not his liberty, for there is always freedom in the desert, nor any visible treasures, for the desert is naked; he will be defending a secret kingdom. Amid the silent waves of sand Bonnafous is captaining his men like a pirate of old, and because of him this encampment at Cape Juby has ceased to be a home to idle shepherds. It is feeling the weight of the storm that is Bonnafous, and because of him the tents are set closer tonight. How the southern silence penetrates the heart: it belongs to Bonnafous! And the old hunter Mouyan is listening to his footsteps in the wind.

When Bonnafous goes home to France, his enemies will not rejoice; they will weep for him, as if his departure has removed one of the poles of their desert and an element of splendour from their existence, and they will ask me:

'Why is your Bonnafous going away?'

'I don't know . . .'

For years on end he has staked his life against theirs. Made their rules his rules. Slept with their stones as a pillow for his head. Through all that ceaseless pursuit, like them, he knew Biblical nights of stars and wind. And now he shows after all, by leaving, that he was not gambling for an essential stake. He just throws in his hand, casually. The Moors he leaves to play alone lose their trust in a meaning for life that does not engage men's flesh and blood. Yet they still want to believe in him:

'Your Bonnafous will come back.'

'I don't know.'

He will come back, they tell themselves. The stakes to be played for in Europe will not satisfy him: not bridge at the garrison, not promotion, not women. Haunted by his lost nobility, he will come back to this land where every step makes the heart beat like a step taken into love. Having imagined that here was mere adventure and back there was the essence, he will discover with nausea that only here did he possess true riches, in the desert: this splendour of the desert night, this silence, this homeland of wind and stars. And if Bonnafous ever comes back, the news will spread far and wide in rebel territory on the very first night. Somewhere in the Sahara the Moors will know that he is sleeping among his two hundred buccaneers. And they will take their dromedaries to the wells in silence. They will make ready their supplies of barley, and check their breech-loaders. Driven by that same hatred, or that same love.

VI

'Hide me in a plane to Marrakesh!'

Night after night, at Juby, a slave of the Moors addressed this brief prayer to me. After which, having done what he could for his life, he would sit down cross-legged and make my tea. At peace for one more day, having confided, as he would see it, in the only doctor who could cure him, and prayed to the only god who could save him. Bent over his kettle now, meditating on the simple images of his life: the black earth of Marrakesh, the pink houses, the elementary belongings of which he had been dispossessed. He bore me no ill-will for my silence, nor for my delay in giving him life: I was not a man in his image but a force to be activated, something akin to a favourable wind which would rise one day upon his destiny.

But as a mere pilot, airport chief for a few months at Cape Juby, blessed with nothing more than a hut against the wall of the Spanish fort and inside the hut with nothing more than a basin, a jug of brackish water and a bed that was too short, I had fewer illusions concerning my power:

'We'll see about that, old Bark.'

All slaves are called Bark, so Bark was his name. In spite of four years in captivity he was not resigned to it yet: he remembered that he had been a king.

'What did you do in Marrakesh, Bark?'

'I was a drover, and my name was Mohammed!'

The chief magistrates themselves would send for him:

'I have bullocks to sell, Mohammed. Go and bring them from the mountain.'

Or at other times:

'I have a thousand sheep on the plain. Take them up to the higher pastures.'

And Bark, armed with an olive-wood sceptre, ruled over their exodus. With sole responsibility for a nation of ewes, slowing down the lively ones for the sake of the lambs to be born and stirring up the stragglers, he strode forward in universal trust and obedience. He alone knew to what promised lands they were climbing, he alone read their course in the stars; filled with a knowledge not shared with the sheep, he alone decided, in his wisdom, the time to rest and the time to drink at the springs. And at night as they slept, filled with tenderness towards such ignorant frailty and bathed in wool up to his knees, Bark, physician and prophet and king, prayed for his people.

One day, some Arabs had approached him:

'Come with us and fetch some animals from the South.'

They had kept him walking for a long time, and three days later, on a track hidden deep in the mountains, a hand was placed on his shoulder. He was baptized Bark, and sold.

I knew other slaves. I used to take tea each day in the tents. Stretched out barefoot on the thick woollen carpet that is the nomad's luxury and the foundation of his dwelling for a few hours, I would savour the day's journey. In the desert you can feel the passage of time. Under the burning of the sun you are on the march towards the evening, towards that cool breeze which will bathe your limbs and wash away all sweat. Under the burning of the sun, men and animals advance towards that great watering place as surely as towards death. So this time of leisure is never wasted. And each day looks as beautiful as the roads that lead to the sea.

I knew those slaves. They enter the tent when the chief has

pulled the stove, the kettle and the glasses from his treasure chest, that chest heavy with absurd objects, with keyless padlocks, flowerless vases, cheap mirrors, old weapons, all washed up here amid the sand and for all the world like the flotsam of a shipwreck.

Then the slave, without a word, fills the stove with dry twigs, blows on the glowing embers, fills the kettle, setting in motion for a girl's task muscles that would uproot a cedar. He is untroubled. Absorbed in the sequence of actions: brew the tea, look after the dromedaries, eat. March under the burning of the day towards the night, and long under the chill of the naked stars for the burning of the day. Happy are the northern lands whose seasons can compose a legend of snow in summer and a legend of sun in winter; sad are the tropics where in the sweating-room nothing really changes, but happy too is this Sahara where day and night swing men so simply from one hope to the other.

Sometimes the black slave squats outside the door, savouring the evening breeze. In his heavy captive body the tide of memory no longer rises. He barely remembers the moment of abduction, the blows, the shouts, the arms that hurled him down into his present darkness. Since that moment he has been sinking into a strange sleep, cut off as if he were a blind man from his slow Senegalese rivers or his white south Moroccan towns, cut off as if he were deaf from familiar voices. This black man is not unhappy, he is crippled. He fell one day into the rhythm of nomadic life. Bound to its migrations, chained for life to the orbits it describes in the desert, what could he now keep in common with a past, with a home, with a wife and children who for him are as dead as the dead?

Men who have lived for years with a great love which they have then lost can grow weary of their lonely nobility. Humbly they reconcile themselves with life, and make their happiness of a commonplace love. They have found a gentle contentment in abdication, in submission, and in entering into the peace of things. The slave creates his pride from his master's burning ember.

'Here, this is for you,' says the chief to the captive, sometimes.

This is the time when the master is good to the slave because of this easing of all fatigues and all burnings, because they enter this coolness side by side. And he grants him a glass of tea. And the captive, bowed down with gratitude for this glass of tea, would kiss the knees of his master. The slave never wears chains. He has so little need of them! He is so faithful! And how wisely he denies the dispossessed black king within him: he is a contented slave now, nothing more.

And yet one day he will be released. When he becomes too old to be worth his food or his clothes, he will be granted an inconceivable freedom. For three days he will offer himself in vain from tent to tent, growing weaker each day, and towards the end of the third day, as compliant as ever, he will lie down on the sand. I have seen them at Juby, naked and dying. The Moors brushed past their death agony, but without cruelty, and the Moorish children played close to the dark wreckage, and ran out playfully each morning to see if it was still moving, but with no mockery of the old servant. It was all within the natural order. It was as if they had said to him: 'You have been a good worker, you have earned the right to go and sleep now.' Stretched out on the ground, he experienced hunger which is mere dizziness, but not injustice which alone is torture. Little by little he became one with the earth. Dried up by the sun and received by the earth. Thirty years of toil, then his right to sleep and to the earth.

When I first came across such a slave, I heard no moan from him: but he had no one against whom to moan. I could sense in him a kind of mysterious acquiescence, like that of the lost, exhausted mountain-dweller who lies down in the snow, wrapping himself in it and in his dreams. It was not his suffering that pained me. He hardly seemed to be suffering. But in the death of a man an unknown world is dying, and I wondered what images were sinking into oblivion with him. What Senegalese plantations, what white Moroccan towns were vanishing. I had no way of knowing whether within that black shape the last light was flickering on paltry concerns: the tea to be brewed, the animals to be taken to the well ... whether a slave's soul was fading into sleep or whether, revived by a tide of memories, mankind lay dying in all his glory. The hard bone of his skull was to my eyes like the old treasure chest. What coloured silks, what images of festivals, what obsolete and pointless vestiges had survived his shipwreck in the desert, I could not know. The chest lay there; it was fastened, and it was heavy. I could not know which place in the world was disintegrating within that man through the immense sleep of his final days, disintegrating in that consciousness and in that flesh which little by little was reverting to root and darkness.

'I was a drover, and my name was Mohammed . . .'

Bark, the black captive, was the first I ever met who resisted. It was unimportant that the Moors had violated his freedom, stripped him in one day more naked than a new-born baby, for God sends storms that ravage within one hour the harvests of men. But more profoundly than in his worldly goods, the Moors had threatened him in his essence as a man. And Bark would not abdicate, when many another captive would have let die within him the poor drover who toiled all year to earn his daily bread!

Bark would not settle into his servitude as some men, weary of waiting, settle into a commonplace happiness. His joys as a slave would not come from the slave-master's moments of kindness. Within his breast he conserved for the absent Mohammed that house where Mohammed had lived, a house that was sad at its emptiness, but which no other would inhabit. Bark was like a white-haired park keeper, dying of faithfulness amid the weeds of the pathways and the tedium of silence.

He would never say: 'I am Mohammed ben Lhaoussin,' but always just: 'My name was Mohammed,' as he dreamed of the day when that forgotten man would come to life again within him, casting away by his very resurrection the outer skin of the slave. Sometimes in the silence of the night all his memories were restored to him in the rich fullness of a song of childhood. 'In the middle of the night,' said our Moorish interpreter, 'in the middle of the night he spoke of Marrakesh, and he wept.' No man living in isolation can escape such homecomings of the mind. Without warning his other self would wake within him, extend through his limbs, seek the wife lying beside him, in that desert where no woman ever came close to Bark; he would listen to the song of the spring water, in that desert where no spring ever flowed. Behind his closed eyes, Bark lived in his mind in a white house, as he sat each night under the same star, out there where men live in houses of cloth and follow the wind. Filled with old affections brought mysteriously alive within him, as if their magnetic pole were close at hand, Bark would come to see me. He wanted to tell me that he was prepared, that all his affections were ready to be given and received, and that all that was needed was the journey home. A sign from me would be enough. And Bark would smile as he told me how it could be done, for no doubt it hadn't occurred to me:

'The mail goes tomorrow. Just hide me in the Agadir plane . . .'

'Poor old Bark!'

How could we help him escape, living as we were in rebel territory? The very next day the Moors would have avenged the robbery and the insult by God knows what massacre. I had tried to buy him, of course, with the help of the airport mechanics – Laubergue, Marchal and Abgrall – but the Moors don't meet European slave-buyers every day, and they took full advantage.

'Twenty thousand francs.'

'What sort of idiots do you take us for?'

'Look at those strong arms of his . . .'

And the months went by.

At last the Moors dropped their price. With the help of friends in France to whom I had written, I found myself in a position to buy old Bark.

The negotiations were quite something. For a week we sat in a circle on the sand, fifteen Moors and I. A friend of the owner was the bandit Zin Ould Rhattari; he was my friend too, and was secretly on my side:

'Sell him. You're going to lose him anyway,' he would say as I had recommended. 'He's sick. You can't see it yet, but he's a sick man inside. One of these days he'll swell up all of a sudden. Sell him right now to the Frenchman.'

I had promised a commission to another bandit, Raggi, if he helped me pull off the sale, and Raggi would tempt the owner:

'With the money you can buy camels and rifles and cartridges. Then you can set off with your men and fight the French, and you'll bring back three or four new young slaves from Atar. Get rid of this old man.'

And Bark was sold to me. I kept him locked up for six days in our hut, for if he had wandered outside before the plane came, the Moors would have captured him again and sold him somewhere else.

But I freed him from his state of slavery. It was a fine ceremony, witnessed by a Muslim holy man, by the former owner and by Ibrahim, the magistrate at Juby. Those three pirates, who would cheerfully have cut off his head twenty yards outside the fortress wall just for the pleasure of putting one over on me, embraced him warmly and signed an official declaration.

'Now you are our son.'

Mine too, according to the law.

And Bark embraced all his fathers.

He lived in a gentle captivity in our hut until the time came to leave. Twenty times a day he asked for a description of the straightforward journey: he would leave the plane at Agadir airport, where he would be given a bus ticket for Marrakesh. Bark was playing at being a free man, as a child plays at being an explorer: going over that journey towards life, the bus, the crowds, the towns he was going to see again . . .

Laubergue came to see me, speaking for Marchal and Abgrall too. Bark mustn't go hungry after his journey. They gave me a thousand francs for him, so that he'd be able to look for work.

Those charitable old ladies who 'do good works' came into my mind, the ones who give twenty francs and demand gratitude. Those aircraft mechanics Laubergue, Marchal and Abgrall were parting with a thousand; it wasn't charity, still less did they want gratitude. Nor were they acting through pity, like those old ladies with their dream of spreading happiness. They were simply contributing to a man's recovery of his human dignity. They knew only too well, as I did, that after the ecstasy of homecoming the first faithful friend waiting on Bark's road would be poverty, and that within three months he would be breaking his back somewhere pulling up railway sleepers. And he would be more unhappy than he had been among us in the desert. But he had the right to be himself, among his own people.

'Come on, old Bark. On your way, and be a man.'

The plane was vibrating, ready for take-off. Bark turned one last time to look at the vast desolation of Cape Juby. Around the plane two hundred Moors had gathered to see what a slave looks like when he stands at the doorway to life. They would pick him up again later, of course, if the plane had to make a forced landing.

We waved farewell to our newborn child of fifty, a little anxious about launching him into the world.

'Goodbye, Bark!'

'No.'

'What do you mean?'

'Not Bark. I am Mohammed ben Lhaoussin.'

The last news we had of him came from Abdallah, the Arab who at our request had looked after him at Agadir.

As the bus did not leave until evening, Bark had a day to fill. He wandered so long and so silently through the little town that Abdallah sensed his discomfort, and asked with concern:

'What's wrong?'

'Nothing . . .'

Suddenly on holiday like this and adrift, Bark could not yet feel his inner resurrection. Certainly there was a muted happiness in him, but apart from that there was no discernible difference between yesterday's Bark and today's. And yet from this very day he shared the daylight equally with other men, and the right to sit here under the shady vault of an Arab café. He did sit, and ordered tea for himself and Abdallah. It was his first act as a sovereign man, and its power ought to have transfigured him. But the waiter poured the tea with no reaction of surprise, as if it were an ordinary act. He did not sense, as he poured the tea, that he was glorifying a free man.

'Let us go somewhere else,' said Bark.

They went up to the Kasbah, on the hill above Agadir.

Little Berber dancing girls approached them, with so much docile sweetness that Bark felt he was coming alive: without knowing it, they were the ones who welcomed him to life. So they took him by the hand and offered him tea, very gracefully, just as they would have offered it to any other man. Bark tried to tell them about his resurrection. They laughed, sweetly, happy for him because he was happy. To fill them with wonder he added: 'I am Mohammed ben Lhaoussin,' but they were unimpressed. Every man has a name, and many come home from so far away . . .

He took Abdallah back towards the town. He wandered among the Jewish stalls, looked at the sea, thought about the fact that he could walk as he pleased in any direction, that he was free . . . But that freedom had a bitter taste, as it revealed to him how few links he had with the world.

And then, as a child passed, Bark gently caressed his cheek. The boy smiled. This was not a master's son to be flattered, but a frail child whose cheek Bark had freely stroked. And who was smiling. That child woke Bark from his sleep, and Bark sensed that he was a little more significant on the earth because of a frail child who had repaid him with a smile. Sensing the beginnings of something, he was striding forward now.

'What are you looking for?' Abdallah asked.

'Nothing,' Bark replied.

But as he turned a corner he came upon a group of children at play, and he stopped. This was it. He looked at them in silence. Then he went off to the Jewish stalls and came back laden with gifts. Abdallah was angry:

'Keep your money, you fool!'

But Bark wasn't listening. Solemnly he called each child to him. And little hands stretched out towards the toys and the bangles and the gold-embroidered slippers. And each child, once his hands were firmly on his treasure, ran away like a savage.

As they heard the news, the other children of Agadir came running: Bark gave them golden slippers to wear. And as the rumour reached the outskirts, so yet more children came shouting and climbing up to the black God, to tug at the old clothes of his slavery and claim their due. Bark was ruining himself.

Abdallah thought he had gone 'crazy with joy'. But for me Bark's behaviour had nothing to do with the sharing of an excess of happiness.

Since he was free, he possessed the essential human wealth: the right to find love, to walk to the north or the south and to earn his bread by his labours. What good was this money . . . What he was experiencing, like a profound hunger, was the need to be a man among men, with ties binding him to other men. The dancers of Agadir had treated old Bark with tenderness, but he had left them as easily as he had come to them; they had no need of him. The Arab waiter, the people in the streets, everyone had respected the free man that he was and shared their sunlight equally with him, but not one had showed that in any sense he needed Bark. He was free but in an infinite way, so that he felt weightless above the earth. He lacked that weight of human relationships that inhibits free movement, those tears and farewells, those reproaches and those joys, everything that a man strokes or tears apart each time he forms a gesture, those thousand chains that bind him to others and make him heavy. But already Bark felt the weight of a thousand hopes . . .

And Bark's reign began in the glory of the sun setting over Agadir, in that coolness which for so long had been the only sweetness, the only place of rest he could expect. And as the time to leave approached Bark moved forward, bathed in that tide of children as once he had been among his ewes, ploughing his first furrow in the world. Tomorrow he would return to the poverty of his own people, responsible for more lives than perhaps his old arms would be able to nourish, but here already he could feel the measure of his true weight. Like an archangel, too airy to live the life of men but finding a way to cheat by sewing lead into his girdle, Bark was straining his way forward, pulled earthward by a thousand children who had such need of golden slippers.

VII

Such is the desert. A Koran, which is only a book of rules for the game, changes its sand into an Empire. Deep in a seemingly empty Sahara a secret drama is being enacted, stirring the passions of men. The true life of the desert lies not in great tribal movements in search of pasture, but in the game being played out there still. What a difference there is in substance between conquered expanses of sand and the rest! And is it not so for all men? Gazing at this transfigured desert, I remember the games of my childhood, that dark and gilded parkland which we peopled with gods, the limitless kingdom which we drew out of that square half mile that we never entirely knew, never entirely explored. We created there a closed civilization where footsteps had a taste and things had a meaning permitted in no other. When we become men, living under other laws, what remains of the shady park of childhood that was so magical, so frozen, so burning, now that we come back and walk in a kind of despair around its little greystone perimeter wall? Amazed to discover within such a tiny enclosure a region of which we had made infinity, we understand that we shall never again enter into that infinity, for it is into the game and not into the park that we would have to enter.

But there is no more rebel territory. No more mystery in the names: Cape Juby, Cisneros, Puerto-Cansado, Saguet-El-Hamra, Dora, Smarra. The horizons of our journeys have faded out one after another, like those insects that lose their colours once caught in the trap of warm hands. But the seekers were not the playthings of an illusion. We were not deluded in our quest for discovery. Nor was the Sultan of the Thousand and One Nights, as he sought an essence so subtle that his beautiful captives died away one by one in his arms at dawn, scarcely touched but with the gold fallen from their wings. We were nourished by the magic of the sands, and now others will perhaps sink their oil-wells there and grow rich on their commerce. But they will have come too late, for those forbidden palm groves and that virgin shell dust gave up to us their most precious essence: they offered just an hour of exaltation, and we are the ones who lived that hour.

It was granted to me once to encounter the desert with my heart. On a flight to Indo-China in 1935 I found myself in Egypt, near the Libyan border. I was stuck in the sands as if in glue, and in those sands I thought my death had come. Here now is that story.

AT THE HEART OF THE DESERT

I

Low cloud greeted me as I came to the Mediterranean, and brought me down to sixty feet. Rain squalls are driving against the windscreen and steam seems to be rising from the sea. I'm straining to see ahead and make sure I don't hit a ship's mast.

André Prévot, my engineer, is lighting cigarettes for me.

'Coffee . . .'

He disappears into the stern of the plane and comes back with the thermos flask. I drink. I flick the throttle from time to time to keep up exactly 2100 revs. I run my eyes over the dials: my subjects are obedient, each needle exactly where it should be. I glance down at the sea, steaming in the rain like a great hot cauldron. If this were a seaplane, I'd be unhappy that it looked so 'hollow', but I'm in an aeroplane. Hollow or not, I can't land on it. And for some unaccountable reason, that gives me an absurd feeling of security. The sea is part of a world that is not my world. An engine failure here is no concern of mine, and doesn't even pose a threat: I'm not rigged for the sea.

After ninety minutes' flying time the rain dies down. The cloud is still very low, but the light is already breaking through it like a great smile. My eyes enjoy this slow preamble to fine weather. Above my head I sense a thin layer of cotton wool, and change course to avoid a squall: no need now to go through the middle of it. And here's the first break in the cloud . . .

I was aware of it before I saw it, for I observe ahead of me on the sea a long, meadow-coloured streak, a kind of oasis of a deep and luminous green, reminiscent of those south Moroccan barley fields that made me catch my breath on my way north from Senegal, after two thousand miles of sand. Here too I have the sense of entering a region a man could live in, and enjoy a lifting of my spirits. I turn to Prévot:

'That's the end of it, we'll be fine now!'
'Yes, fine . . .'

Tunis. I'm signing papers during refuelling. But just as I come out of the office I hear a sound like the splash of a diver. One of those cushioned sounds, with no echo. Instantaneously I remember a similar sound: an explosion in a garage. Two men had died of that hoarse cough. I turn towards the road that runs beside the runway: a little cloud of smoking dust, where two cars have crashed at speed, suddenly immobilized as if in ice. Men are running towards them, others towards us:

'The phone . . . Get a doctor . . . His head . . .'

My heart tightens. In the peaceful light of evening, fate has carried out a successful raid. A beauty destroyed, or an intelligence, or a life . . . Just like the bandits as they moved about the desert, with no one hearing their supple steps on the sand. That's how it came, the brief sound of the raid on the camp. Then everything returned to the same gilded silence, the same peace . . . Someone close to me is talking about a fractured skull. I don't want to know about that lifeless, bleeding forehead. I turn my back on the road and climb into my plane. But in my heart I am carrying a sense of threat. I'll recognize that sound in a while. When I scrape my black plateau at a hundred and seventy miles an hour I'll recognize that same hoarse cough: that same grunt of destiny keeping its appointment with us.

And on to Benghazi.

II

On we go. Two hours of daylight left. My sunglasses are already off as I fly into Tripolitania. And the sand is turning golden. God, how empty this planet is! Once more, the rivers and the shady woods and the habitations of men seem to exist through conjunctions of happy chance. There is so much rock and sand!

But all of that is foreign to me, for I live in the realm of flight. I can sense the coming of night, in which I will be enclosed as in a temple. Enclosed with the secrets of fundamental rites, in a meditation that is beyond help. Already this profane world is fading, and it will vanish entirely. The whole landscape is still nourished with golden light, but already something is evaporating from it. And I know nothing, absolutely nothing, to rival this time of day. Those who have experienced the inexpressible love of flying will understand me fully.

Little by little, then, I am giving up the sunlight. I give up the broad golden surfaces that would have welcomed me if my engines had failed . . . I give up the landmarks that would have guided me. I give up the outlines of the mountains against the sky that would have warned me of dangers ahead. I am entering the night. Sailing. Nothing left to me now but the stars . . .

This death of the world takes place slowly. Little by little, I am abandoned by light. The earth and sky merge gradually. The earth rises and seems to spread like a mist. The first stars tremble as if shimmering in green water. It will be a long time yet before they harden into diamonds. And still longer before I can witness the silent games of the shooting stars. Deep in the heart of some nights, I have seen so many racing sparks that it seemed as if a great wind were blowing among the stars.

Prévot is testing the permanent lights and the emergency lamps. We wrap the bulbs in red paper.

'Another layer . . .'

He adds another thickness and touches a switch. The light is still too bright. As in a photographer's darkroom, it would obscure our pale image of the external world. It would destroy that slight fleshiness which things still have, sometimes, at night. That darkness has now come, but not yet in its true life, for a crescent moon survives. Prévot plunges into the stern and returns with a sandwich. I nibble at a bunch of grapes. I'm not hungry. Neither hungry nor thirsty. I feel no fatigue, and it seems to me that I could fly on like this for ten years.

The moon is dead.

Approaching Benghazi now, in pitch darkness. Benghazi lies in such a deep, dark hollow that there is no halo of light above it. Only as I reached the town did I see it. I've been looking for the airfield, but now they've switched its red beacons on. The lights form a rectangle against the blackness. I turn. The beam of a beacon pointed to the sky rises like the jet of a fire hose, then swings around and traces a golden pathway across the airfield. I bank again to get a good view of any obstacles. The night-landing facilities at this field are admirable. I reduce my speed and begin to drop like a diver into black water.

I land at 23.00 hours, local time, and taxi towards the beacon. The most courteous officers and soldiers in the world move in and out of the darkness and the harsh floodlight, alternately visible and invisible. They take my papers and begin refuelling. Everything will be taken care of within twenty minutes.

'Circle over us, or we won't know if you've taken off all right.'

On we go.

I taxi along that golden road towards my open gateway to the sky. My Simoun aircraft lifts her overload well within the take-off space available. The searchlight follows me, making it hard to turn, but finally it releases me as they realize it was dazzling me. I bank vertically to circle around and the light hits me in the face again, but the instant it has touched me it swings away and aims its long golden flute elsewhere. I can sense real consideration for me in these actions, as I bank again towards the desert.

The weather stations in Paris, Tunis and Benghazi have forecast a following wind of twenty to twenty-five miles an hour. I can count on a cruising speed of a hundred and ninety miles an hour. I set my course for the middle of the right-hand sector between Alexandria and Cairo, thus avoiding the prohibited coastal zones. Whatever sideways drift might occur without my knowledge, I'll be able to hang on to the lights of one of those cities to right or left, or more generally to those of the Nile valley. I'll be flying for three hours twenty minutes if the wind speed remains constant, three hours forty-five if it drops. And I begin to absorb six hundred and fifty miles of desert.

No moon now. Black asphalt distended to the stars. I will see no light, benefit from no landmark, and with no radio I will receive no human signal until I reach the Nile. There is no point in looking at anything other than my compass and my artificial horizon. Nothing interests me now but the slow breathing of a narrow line of radium on the dark background of the instrument screen. Whenever Prévot moves I gently correct the shifts in alignment. I lift the plane to six and a half thousand feet, where I have been told the winds are favourable. At long intervals I switch on a light to look at the engine dials, not all of which are luminous, but for the most part I am wrapped in darkness, among my miniature constellations which give off the same mineral glow as the stars, the same inexhaustible and secret light, and which speak the same language. Like the astronomers, I too am reading in a book of celestial mechanics. Like them I feel studious and uncorrupted. Everything in the external world is eclipsed. Prévot has fallen asleep now after long resistance, and I savour my solitude all the more. The engine drones on gently and in front of me, on the instrument panel, there are all those peaceful stars.

Yet I am deep in thought. We have neither moonlight nor radio to help us. No link, however slender, will bind us to the world now until we fly into the thread of light that will be the Nile. We are outside the world, and our engine alone suspends us and sustains us in this asphalt. We are travelling through the great dark valley of legend, the valley of ordeal. There is no help here. No forgiveness for errors. We are in the hands of God's discretion.

A ray of light is escaping from a joint in the lamp shaft. I wake Prévot so that he can deal with it. Prévot stirs in the shadows like a bear, shakes himself awake, and moves forward. He is engrossed with some combination of handkerchiefs and black paper, and now the ray of light has gone. It broke incongruously into this world, for it was of a different quality from the pale and remote gleam of the radium. A night-club light, not a shining star. But above all it was dazzling me, eclipsing the other lights.

Three hours have passed. A sudden brightness flashes on my starboard side. I look out, and see a long trail of light streaming back from my wing-tip lamp, which until now has been invisible. An intermittent gleam, now intense, now subdued: I'm flying into a cloud, which is reflecting my lamp. Coming close to my landmarks as I am now, I would have appreciated a clear sky. The wing gleams under its halo. The light settles on it now, becomes constant in its radiance, and forms a pink bouquet. Strong turbulence swings me sideways. I'm flying somewhere in the eddies of a cumulus, with no idea of its density. I lift the plane to eight thousand and I'm still in it. The bouquet of flowers is still there, motionless and growing ever brighter. Right. Fine. Nothing to be done. Think of something else. We'll see well enough when we're out of it. But I dislike this louche tavern light.

I assess the situation: 'I'm bouncing around here a bit, and that's to be expected, but there's been turbulence all the way in spite of a clear sky and my altitude. The wind hasn't dropped, and I must be doing more than a hundred and ninety miles an hour.' I'm not really clear about anything, though, and I'll try to take my bearings when I'm out of the cloud.

And out we come. The bouquet has suddenly vanished, signalling the change. I look ahead and see, in as much as I can see anything at all, a narrow valley of sky and the wall of the next cumulus. The bouquet is already alight again.

Just a few seconds' freedom from that mess, then. After three and half hours' flying time it's beginning to bother me, for if I'm progressing as anticipated I must be approaching the Nile. If I'm lucky I may see it down one of the breaks, but there are few of those. I don't dare reduce my height yet: if by chance I've been slower than I think, I'm flying over high ground.

I still feel no anxiety, just a fear that I may be losing time. But I set a limit for my serenity: four hours fifteen minutes. After that much flying time and even in the unlikely event of zero wind, I will definitely have crossed the Nile valley.

As I reach the fringe of the cloud, the bouquet flashes on and off more and more rapidly, then suddenly goes out. I am not enjoying these coded communications with the demons of the night.

A green star emerges ahead of me, shining like a lighthouse. Is it a star, or is it a beacon? I don't like this supernatural gleam either, this Magi-star, this dangerous invitation.

Prévot is awake now, shining a light on the engine dials. I wave him and his torch away. I have just flown into a clear space between two clouds, and use the opportunity to look down. Prévot is going back to sleep.

There's nothing to look at in any case.

Four hours five minutes. Prévot has come to sit beside me:

'We ought to be nearing Cairo . . .'

'I reckon so . . .'

'Is that a star out there, or a beacon?'

I have throttled down a little. That's probably what woke Prévot. He is sensitive to every variation of sound in flight. I begin a slow descent, to slip out beneath the cloud mass.

A look at the map has told me that I must be over land at sea level: no danger of flying into a hill. Still descending, I turn and head due north, so that the lights of the cities will shine in my windows. I must have flown past them, so they ought to appear on the left. Now I'm flying under the cumulus, but skirting another cloud hanging lower down to my left. I bank away to avoid being caught in its net, and head north-north-east.

That cloud undoubtedly goes deeper, for it is masking the whole horizon. I dare not lose any more height. My altimeter is down to the 1300 feet mark, but I don't know the atmospheric pressure here. Prévot leans forward and I shout: 'I'm going to head for the sea. I'd rather come down there if I have to than crash here . . .'

In fact there's nothing to prove that I haven't already drifted out over the sea. The visibility under that cloud is precisely nil. I press my face to the window, trying to read what is beneath me, trying to find lights or signs. I am a man raking through ashes, a man struggling to find the embers of life in the bottom of a fireplace.

'A lighthouse!'

We saw it simultaneously, that flashing decoy! What madness! Where was that phantom beacon, that invention of the night? For it was at the very second when Prévot and I were straining forward to find it once more, a thousand feet under our wings, that suddenly . . .

'Ah!'

I don't believe I said anything else. I don't believe I felt anything except a tremendous impact that shook the very foundations of our world. We crashed into the ground, at one hundred and seventy miles an hour.

I don't believe I expected anything, in the split second that followed, but the great crimson star of the explosion that would blow the two of us into indistinguishable pieces. Neither Prévot nor I felt the slightest emotion. Within myself I was conscious only of an inordinate sense of expectation as I waited for that dazzling star which was to obliterate us within that second. But there was no crimson star. There was a kind of earthquake that shattered our cabin, ripping out the windows, flinging metal panels a hundred yards, filling our very entrails with its roar. The plane was quivering like a knife hurled into a hard block of wood. And we were pummelled by that anger. One second, two seconds ... The plane was still quivering and I was waiting with grotesque impatience for its power supply to blow it apart like a grenade. But the underground tremors went on, with no final eruption. And I could grasp nothing of these invisible workings, nothing of this quaking, this anger, this interminable waiting ... five seconds, six seconds ... Suddenly we felt ourselves spinning, then a shock that hurled our cigarettes out of the window and smashed the starboard wing, then nothing. Nothing but a frozen immobility. I yelled at Prévot:

'Jump! Now!'

At the same moment he was shouting:

'Fire!'

We had already swung ourselves out where the window had been, and were standing twenty yards from the plane. I was asking Prévot:

'Are you hurt?'

'Not a scratch!' he replied. But he was rubbing his knee.

'Check yourself all over,' I said, 'move everything, and swear there's nothing broken ...'

'It's nothing,' he answered, 'just that emergency pump ...'

I was sure he was about to keel over at any moment, split apart from head to navel, but he kept on saying, with his eyes fixed in a stare:

'It was that emergency pump!'

He's gone crazy, I was thinking, he'll start dancing in a minute ...

But he turned his eyes away at last from the plane, which was not going to burn now, looked at me and said once more:

'I'm all right. It's just that emergency pump, it caught me on the knee.'

III

We are alive, and it makes no sense. Torch in hand, I retrace the plane's path along the ground. Three hundred yards back from where we came to rest there are already panels and twisted pieces of metal; the sand is spattered with them all along its course. When daylight comes, we shall know that we have flown almost tangentially into a gentle slope at the top of an empty plateau. At the point of impact there is a hole in the sand as if a plough had been dug into it. Without somersaulting, the plane slid on its belly with the anger and the tail-lashings of a reptile, slid on its belly at one hundred and seventy miles an hour. It seems we owe our lives to these round black pebbles that roll freely on the sand; they made a tray of marbles for us.

Prévot disconnects the batteries to prevent a delayed-action short-circuit and fire. Leaning against the engine, I reflect: perhaps at altitude there may have been a following wind of thirty miles an hour, for four and a quarter hours; I certainly was buffeted about. But if it changed after the forecast, I have no idea of its new direction. So all I know is that I am within a square, each of whose sides measures two hundred and fifty miles.

Prévot comes and sits beside me, saying:

'I can't believe we're alive . . .'

I say nothing in reply, and I feel no joy. A little notion has made its way into my head and is itching in there already.

Asking Prévot to light his lamp as a landmark, I set off in a straight line with my torch in my hand, examining the ground minutely. I move forward slowly, describe a wide arc, change direction several times, scrutinizing the ground as if hunting for a lost ring. A little while ago I was searching for the glowing ember, in just the same way. On I go in the darkness, bent over the moving white disc. Just as I thought . . . just as I thought . . . I climb slowly back up to the plane. I sit by the cabin, deep in thought. I was looking for a reason to hope, and did not find it. I was looking for a sign offered by life, and life gave me no sign.

'Prévot, I didn't see a single blade of grass . . .'

Prévot says nothing, and I don't know if he has understood. We'll talk about it again when the curtain goes up, when daylight comes. All I feel now is a great weariness, as I think: 'Two hundred and fifty miles, give or take, in the desert! . . .' Suddenly I leap to my feet:

'Our water!'

Petrol and oil tanks burst, water supplies too. The sand has drunk it all. We find a pint of coffee in the bottom of a battered thermos, and half a pint of wine in another. We filter these liquids, and mix them. We find a few grapes too, and an orange. I calculate: 'We'll use that up in five hours, walking in the desert sun . . .'

We settle down in the cabin to wait for daylight. I stretch out, intending to sleep. As I grow drowsy I take stock: we have no idea of our position. We have less than a quart of liquid. If we are more or less on course they'll find us within a week; that's the best we can hope for, and it'll be too late. If we have drifted off course, they'll find us in six months. We can't count on a plane finding us: they'll have two thousand miles to cover.

'It's a pity, you know . . .' says Prévot.

'What is?'

'We could have got it over with in one moment! . . .'

But you can't give up so quickly. Prévot and I pull ourselves together. We mustn't lose the chance, however slight it may be, of a miraculous rescue by air. Nor can we afford to stay put, and perhaps miss a nearby oasis. Today we will walk, all day, and then return to our machine. And before we leave, we will inscribe our plan in huge letters on the sand.

Curled up now, I shall sleep until dawn. And I am happy to sleep, as my fatigue wraps me in a multiple presence. I am not alone in the desert, for my semi-sleep is peopled with voices, with memories, with whispered secrets. I am not thirsty yet, and I abandon myself to sleep as to a journey into the unknown. Reality is losing ground to dreams . . .

Ah, it was so different when the daylight came!

IV

I have had a great love for the Sahara. I have spent nights in rebel territory, and have woken in that vast golden expanse shaped by the wind like the swell of the sea. I have waited for rescue, sleeping under my wing, but it was not like this.

We are walking along the slopes of rounded hills. The ground is sand, entirely covered with a single layer of shining black pebbles. It is as if we are walking on scales of metal, and all the domes around us shine like armour. We have fallen into a metallic world. We are locked in an iron landscape.

We reach the top of the first crest, and see beyond it another just the same, black and shining. As we walk we scrape the ground with our feet, marking out a guiding thread for our return later. We are walking into the sun. I have decided to head east against all logic, for everything would indicate that I did cross the Nile: the weather forecast, my flight time. But I ventured briefly westward, and felt an inexplicable sense of unease. So I have put off the west until tomorrow. And I have provisionally sacrificed the north, though the sea lies that way. Three days from now, when in semi-delirium we will decide to abandon our machine for good and to walk straight ahead until we drop, the east will again be our direction. Or more exactly east-north-east. That too will be against all reason, and against all hope. And after our rescue we will discover that no other direction would have brought us home, for a northward trek would have exhausted us, and we would not have reached the sea. However absurd it may appear, it seems to me today that in the absence of any other influence on our decision, I chose that direction for the simple reason that it had saved my friend Guillaumet in the Andes, where I had searched for him so far and wide. In some obscure way, it had become for me the direction of life.

After five hours the landscape changes. A river of sand seems to flow along a valley, and we follow this valley floor, striding forward to cover the greatest distance before returning to the plane if we find nothing. Suddenly I come to a halt:

'Prévot.'

'What?'

'Our tracks . . .'

How long ago did we forget to leave a furrow behind us? If we cannot find it, we shall die.

We turn around but bear away to the right. After some distance we will cut across at right angles to our original direction and connect with our track where we were still marking it.

Having retied that thread, we are on our way again. The heat is rising, and with it come the mirages. Just simple mirages at this stage. Great lakes form and then evaporate as we approach. We decide to cross the valley of sand, and to scale the highest dome to scan the horizon. We have already been walking for six hours. In great strides, we must have covered more than twenty miles. Reaching the summit of this black hump, we sit down in silence. At our feet, our valley of sand opens out into a desert of stoneless sand, and its dazzling brightness scorches our eyes. Emptiness, as far as the eye can see. But on the horizon the play of light is forming more disturbing mirages: fortresses and minarets, angular geometric shapes. There is a great dark patch of sham vegetation, overhung by the last of the clouds that dissolve by day and are reborn at night. It is merely the shadow of a cumulus.

There is no point in going on. This attempt will take us nowhere. We have to return to our plane, that red and white beacon that may be spotted by our comrades. I can build no hopes on their search, but it does seem the only possibility of salvation. Most importantly of all, we have left our last drops of liquid there, and already our need to drink them is absolute. We have to go back if we are to live.

But how hard it is to turn back when we might be walking towards life! Beyond the mirages, perhaps the horizon is indeed rich in real cities, in conduits of sweet water and in meadows. I know I am right to turn back. And yet I have the feeling that I am capsizing, as I give that terrible push to the tiller.

We are lying down near the plane, after covering forty miles. Our liquid is finished. We saw nothing to the east, and no comrade has flown over this landscape. How long will we hold out? Such thirst, already . . .

We have built a great pyre with some wreckage from the splintered wing. The petrol was ready, and the sheets of magnesium that give off a hard white light. We waited for full darkness before lighting our fire . . . But where are the men to see it?

Now the flames are rising. Reverently, we watch our beacon burning in the desert, our silent and shining message radiating into the night. The thought comes to me that if it is certainly carrying an appeal full of pathos, it is also carrying a great deal of love. May another fire be lit in the darkness: only men have fire, let them answer us!

I see the eyes of my wife. Only those eyes, nothing more. Questioning me. I see the eyes of all those who perhaps care for me. All questioning. A whole assembly of eyes, reproaching me for my silence. I am answering! I am answering! I am answering with all my strength, I can hurl no brighter flame into the darkness!

I have done what I could. We have done what we could: forty miles with barely a drop to drink. Now we have no more to drink. Is it our fault if we cannot just sit and wait? We could have stayed here, like good children, sucking at our flasks, but from the moment when I inhaled the bottom of the tin beaker, a clock began to tick. From the second when I sucked in the last drop, I began to descend a slope. Can I help it if time is carrying me away like a river? Prévot is weeping. I put a hand on his shoulder, and say, to console him:

'If we're screwed, we're screwed . . .'

And he answers:

'You think I'm crying for myself . . . ?'

No, of course, I have already learnt this truth. Nothing is unbearable. Tomorrow, and the day after tomorrow, I shall learn definitively that nothing is unbearable. I only half believe in torture. My thoughts on this are already formed. I thought one day that I was drowning, imprisoned in a cockpit, and I did not suffer much. Sometimes I have expected to be smashed to pieces, and it did not seem a significant event. Here too, I shall feel little anguish. Tomorrow I shall learn stranger things yet about this. And God alone knows whether, in spite of my great fire, I have given up trying to make men hear me! . . .

'You think I'm crying for myself . . . ?' Yes, yes, that's what is unbearable. Every time I see those expectant eyes, I feel a burning. Suddenly I feel like leaping up and running straight ahead. They're crying for help out there, they're sinking!

It is a strange reversal of roles, but I have already found it to be so. And yet I needed Prévot to convince me of it finally. Well, Prévot too will not experience that anguish in the face of death that people prattle on about endlessly. But there is something that neither he nor I can bear.

Oh, I can readily accept sleep, sleep for a night or for centuries. If I'm asleep I don't know the difference. And what peace! But those cries from over there, those great flames of despair . . . I can't bear the image. I can't just fold my arms in the face of those shipwrecks! Every second of silence is murdering something in those I love. And a great rage is surging within me: why these chains, preventing me from arriving in time and rescuing those who are drowning? Why is our fire not carrying our cry to the ends of the earth? Be patient! . . . We're coming! . . . We're coming! . . . We'll save you!

The magnesium is burnt off now, and our fire is turning red. There is nothing here but a pile of embers, and we are hunched over them for warmth. Our great shining message is finished. What has it set in motion in the world? Nothing, I know it well enough. It was a prayer that could not be heard.

That's how it is. I'll sleep now.

V

At daybreak, wiping the wings with a rag, we gathered a little dew mixed with paint and oil. It was nauseating, but we drank it. There was nothing else, and at least we've moistened our lips. After this banquet, Prévot says:

'It's lucky we've got the revolver.'

Suddenly aggressive, I turn towards him, filled with vicious hostility. I would hate nothing so much at this moment as a gush of emotion. I have an overwhelming need to see everything in straightforward terms. To be born is straightforward. To grow up is straightforward. And to die of thirst is straightforward.

Now I'm watching Prévot out of the corner of my eye, ready to hurt his feelings if that's what it takes to shut him up. But Prévot's words were spoken without emotion. He was dealing with a matter of hygiene, approaching the subject as if saying: 'We ought to wash our hands.' So we are of one mind. I thought about it yesterday, in fact, when I spotted the leather holster. My thoughts were rational, not born of emotion. Pathos arises only in our social being. In our powerlessness to reassure those for whom we are responsible. And not in the revolver.

They are not searching for us yet, or, to be more precise, they are searching elsewhere for us. Probably in Arabia. And in fact we shall hear no plane until tomorrow, after abandoning our own. And that single distant flight will mean nothing to us. Black specks mingled with a thousand black specks in the desert, we cannot expect to be seen. Thoughts on this torture will be attributed to me; none of them will be true. I will suffer no torture. The rescuers will seem to be orbiting in another universe.

It takes two weeks of searching to find a plane, in about two thousand miles of desert, when you have no information: they are probably looking for us from Tripolitania to Persia. Yet even today I am clinging to this slender possibility, for there is no other. I change tactic, deciding to explore on my own. Prévot will prepare a fire and light it if anyone turns up, but no one will turn up.

So I head off, not even knowing if I will have the strength to return. Back into my memory comes all I know of the Libyan desert. In the Sahara humidity is a constant 40 per cent, but here it drops to 18 per cent. And life evaporates like a haze. Bedouin tribesmen, travellers and colonial officials all teach that a man can last for nineteen hours without water. After twenty hours his eyes flood with light, and it is the beginning of the end: thirst's onslaught is devastating.

Yet this north-easterly wind, this abnormal wind that deceived us and defied all forecasts when it marooned us on this plateau, may well be sustaining us now. But for how long will it grant us this reprieve, before the first light in the eyes?

So I head off, as if setting out in a canoe to cross the ocean.

Yet in the dawn light the setting seems less deathly, and I start out with my hands in my pockets, like a thief on the prowl. Last night we set snares at the mouths of some mysterious burrows, and the poacher within me is waking. I check the traps: they are empty.

So I will drink no blood. To tell the truth, I hadn't expected to.

Far from being disappointed, my curiosity is aroused. What do these desert animals live on? They must be fennecs, little carnivorous sand-foxes the size of rabbits, with enormous ears. I can't resist the desire to follow the track of one of them. It leads me to a narrow river of sand where each print is clearly outlined. I admire the pretty palm-shape formed by the three fanned toes. I can imagine my friend trotting along gently at dawn, licking the dew from the stones. The tracks are spaced more widely now: my fennec broke into a run here. Then a companion joined him, and they trotted side by side. There is a strange thrill in being part of this morning stroll. I love these signs of life. And I forget my thirst for a moment . . .

At last I reach my foxes' larder. Every hundred yards or so, a tiny dry shrub the size of a soup tureen emerges from the sand, its stalks heavy with little golden snails. The fennec goes shopping at dawn. And here I come face to face with a great mystery of nature.

My friend the fennec doesn't stop at every bush. There are some, laden with snails, that he disdains. Others he walks around with evident caution. He does go to some, but without stripping them bare. He takes two or three shells, then moves to another restaurant.

Is he playing a game, not appeasing his hunger all at once, to make the pleasure of his morning stroll more lasting? I don't think so. This game coincides too well with an essential strategy. If the fennec gorged himself on the products of the first bush, he would strip it bare in two or three meals of its living cargo. And as he went from bush to bush he would wipe out his stock. But the fennec is careful not to upset the breeding cycle. Not only does he go to a hundred of these brown tufts for a single meal, but he never lifts two neighbouring shells from the same branch. It all takes place as if he is conscious of the danger. If he ate his fill without consideration, there would be no more snails. No more snails, and no more fennecs.

The trail brings me back to the burrow. No doubt he's down there listening to me, terrified by the rumble of my footsteps. And I say to him: 'Little fox, I've had it. But it's a strange thing, it hasn't stopped me taking an interest in your state of mind . . .'

I stand there lost in thought. It seems to me that you can adapt to anything. The idea that he may die thirty years later doesn't spoil a man's pleasures. Thirty years, or three days . . . it's a question of perspective.

But certain images must be forgotten . . .

*

I am moving on again now, and in my weariness something is already altering within me. If there are no mirages here, I am inventing them . . .

'Hey there!'

I raise my arms and shout, but that beckoning man was just a black rock. Everything is coming to life in the desert. I just tried to wake that sleeping Bedouin, and he turned into a black tree trunk. A tree trunk? A surprising presence here. I bend to examine it, and try to lift a broken branch: it's made of marble! I straighten up and look around me; I see more black lumps of marble. An antediluvian forest, littering the ground with its broken columns. It came crashing down like a cathedral, a hundred thousand years ago, destroyed by a hurricane in the time of Genesis. And the centuries have brought to my feet these sections of giant columns, polished like steel components, petrified, vitrified, the colour of ink. I can see the knots of their branches and the torsions of life in them, I can count the trunk rings. This forest, once filled with birds and with music, has been struck with a curse and turned to salt. And I sense the hostility of this landscape. Blacker than the iron armour of the hills, these solemn ruins reject me. What place do I have here, living as I am, among this incorruptible marble? Perishable as I am, with my body that will be dissolved, what place do I have here in this eternity?

I have already covered about fifty miles since yesterday. This dizziness must be due to my thirst. Or the sun. It gleams on these columns, which seem to have been glazed with oil. It gleams on this universal carapace. There is no sand here. No foxes. Nothing but a giant anvil, and I am walking upon that anvil, feeling the reverberation of the sun inside my head . . .

'Hey! Hey there!'

'There's nothing there. Calm down, You're delirious.'

Here I am, talking to myself, appealing to reason as I must. It's so hard to reject what my eyes are seeing, so hard not to run towards that moving caravan . . . there . . . look!

'Idiot. You know you're inventing it . . .'

'Then nothing in the world is real . . .'

*

Nothing is real except that cross, on that hill twelve miles away. That cross, or that lighthouse . . .

But the sea isn't that way. So it's a cross. I've been studying the map all night. Pointlessly, for my position is unknown. But I pored over all signs of human presence, and somewhere I found a small circle, surmounted by a cross like this one. Turning to the legend, I read: 'Religious establishment'. Beside the cross I saw a black dot, and the legend told me: 'Permanent well'. My heart missed a beat, and I read aloud the words: 'Permanent well . . . permanent well . . . permanent well!' What price Ali-Baba's treasures against a permanent well! A little further on I observed two white circles, and read on the legend: 'Intermittent well'. Rather less inspiring. Then, all around them, nothing. Absolutely nothing.

But there it is, my religious establishment! The monks have raised a cross on the hill as a sign to the shipwrecked! I only have to walk towards it. And run up to those Dominicans . . .

'There are only Coptic monasteries in Libya.'

'. . . to those studious Dominicans. They have a beautiful cool kitchen with red tiles, and out in the yard a wonderful rusted pump. Under the rusted pump, under the rusted pump, you've guessed it . . . under the rusted pump is the permanent well! Oh! What rejoicing when I ring at their gate, when I pull on the great bell . . .'

'Idiot, you're talking about a house in Provence, and it hasn't got a bell.'

'. . . when I pull on the great bell! The porter will raise his arms to heaven and cry out: "You have been sent from God!" and he will summon all the monks. And they'll come running. And they'll welcome me like a destitute child. They'll lead me to the kitchen. And they'll say: "A moment, wait a moment, my son . . . we're sending someone to the permanent well . . ." '

And I will be trembling with happiness . . .

No, I will not weep just because there is no cross now on the hilltop.

What was promising in the west is merely a lie. I turn due north.

The north, at least, is filled with the song of the sea.

At the top of this ridge, see how the horizon spreads! And there, the most beautiful city in the world.

'You know it's a mirage . . .'

I know it's a mirage. You can't fool me! But suppose I feel like plunging into a mirage? Suppose I want to feel hope? Suppose I find pleasure in that crenellated town, all decked out in sunlight? Suppose I choose to walk straight ahead with a spring in my step, for I feel no fatigue now, and I'm happy . . . Prévot and his revolver, what a laugh! I prefer my drunkenness. I'm drunk. I'm dying of thirst!

The evening light has sobered me. I have come to a sudden halt, frightened as I sense how far I have travelled. In the twilight the mirage is dying. The horizon has stripped itself of its splendour, its palaces, its priestly vestments. It is a desert horizon.

'You've covered some ground! You'll be caught in the darkness, you'll have to wait for daybreak, and tomorrow your tracks will be wiped out and you'll be nowhere.'

'So I may as well keep walking straight ahead . . . What's the point of turning back? Don't make me bring the ship round when perhaps my arms were about to open, were even now opening to the sea . . .'

'Where have you seen the sea? You'll never reach it anyway. It's probably two hundred miles away. And Prévot is watching for you by the Simoun! Perhaps he's been spotted by a caravan . . .'

Yes, I'll turn back, but first I'm going to shout for men to hear:

'Hey!'

Good God, this planet has people on it . . .

'Hey there! Mankind . . . !'

I am hoarse. No voice left. I feel ridiculous, shouting like this . . . I yell once more:

'Mankind!'

Pompous and pretentious, the word echoes.

And I turn back.

After two hours of walking, I see the flames which Prévot, in his panic at thinking me lost, has launched into the sky . . . Oh! How little I care . . . .

Another hour's walk . . . Five hundred yards now. A hundred yards. Fifty.

'Ah!'

I have stopped in my tracks, amazed. Joy is filling my heart, I am fighting to contain its violence. In the firelight, Prévot is talking with two Arabs as they lean against the engine. He hasn't seen me yet. He is too absorbed in his own joy. Oh, if only I'd waited like him . . . I'd be saved already! I cry out ecstatically:

'Hey!'

The two Bedouin give a start and look at me. Prévot leaves them there and comes forward to meet me. I open my arms, and Prévot catches me by the elbow. Did he think I was going to fall? I say to him:

'We're saved at last, then!'

'What do you mean?'

'The Arabs!'

'What Arabs?'

'Those Arabs, there, with you! . . .'

Prévot looks at me strangely, and speaks as if revealing a secret to me with a heavy heart:

'There are no Arabs . . .'

This time, most likely, I will weep.

VI

A man can live here for nineteen hours without water, and yet what have we drunk since last night? A few drops of dew at daybreak! But the wind is still coming from the north-east and slowing down our evaporation. That shield is still encouraging high cloud formations in the sky. If only they would drift towards us, if only it would rain! But it never rains in the desert.

'Prévot, let's cut a parachute into triangles. We'll weight the sections on the ground with stones. And if the wind doesn't change, we'll gather the dew at daybreak in one of our petrol tanks, by wringing out the material.'

We have laid out the six white panels under the stars, and Prévot has ripped a tank out of the plane. Nothing to do now but wait for daylight.

In the wreckage, Prévot has discovered a miraculous orange. We are sharing it. It is little enough when what we need is a couple of gallons of water, but I am overwhelmed by it.

Lying beside our nocturnal fire I am looking at this shining fruit, saying to myself: 'Men don't know what an orange is . . .' And my thoughts continue: 'We're condemned to death, and yet again that certainty doesn't deny me my pleasure. This half of an orange held tight in my hand is giving me one of the greatest joys of my life . . .' I lie on my back and suck the fruit, counting the shooting stars. For a moment, my happiness is infinite. And I think: 'We cannot read the world in whose order we are living, if we are not ourselves locked within it.' Only today do I understand the condemned man's cigarette and glass of rum. I could not come to terms with his acceptance of those paltry gifts. And yet he draws great pleasure from them. If he smiles, people think he is brave. But he is smiling as he drinks his rum. What they do not grasp is that his perspective has shifted, and that out of his final hour he has created a human life.

We have gathered a vast quantity of water! Perhaps two quarts. No more thirst! We're saved, we can drink now!

I dip my tin mug fully into the tank, but the water is a delightful greenish yellow colour. The first mouthful has such an appalling taste that I have to catch my breath before completing the swallow, in spite of my tormenting thirst. I could easily drink mud, but this taste of poisonous metal is stronger than my thirst.

I look at Prévot who is turning round and round, staring downwards as if searching carefully for something. Suddenly he bends over and vomits, still rotating. Thirty seconds later, it's my turn. The stomach cramps drive me to my knees, with my fingers digging into the sand. Without a word, we remain like that for a quarter of an hour, convulsed, bringing up nothing but a little bile.

It's over. Now I feel just a distant nausea. But our last hope is gone. I cannot say whether our defeat is due to some coating on the parachute or to the deposit of carbon tetrachloride that forms on the tank. We should have had some other receptacle, some other cloth.

So let's get going! It's daylight. Time to move! We're going to get off this cursed plateau and stride out straight ahead until we drop. Guillaumet in the Andes is my example: I've been thinking about him a lot since yesterday. I am going to disobey our formal instruction, which is to stay close to the wreck. No one is going to come and find us here.

Once more we discover that it is not we who are shipwrecked, but those who are waiting for us! Those who are threatened by our silence. Those already torn apart by a terrible miscalculation. Not to set our course towards them would be unthinkable. Guillaumet too, when he came down from the Andes, told me that he was heading towards the victims! This truth is universal.

'If I were alone in the world,' says Prévot, 'I would just lie down.'

And we walk straight ahead, east-north-east. If we are beyond the Nile, every step is taking us deeper into the density of the Arabian desert.

I remember nothing now of that day. I remember only my urge to hurry. My haste towards something, anything, collapse. I remember too that I walked with my eyes on the ground, for the mirages were too much to stomach. From time to time we checked our course with the compass, and we lay down to catch our breath a little. Somewhere I threw away my waterproof coat, which I was keeping for the night. That's all I know. My memories come together again only with the coolness of evening. I too had become like the sand, and everything within me was featureless.

At sunset, we decide to make camp. I know full well that we should keep moving: this night without water will be the end of us. But we have brought along the pieces of parachute cloth, and if the poison is not in the coating we might be able to drink something in the morning. Once more we must stretch out our dew-traps under the stars.

But to the north, the evening sky is cloudless. And the taste of the wind is different. So is its direction. Already the warm breath of the desert is touching us. The beast awakes! I can feel it licking our hands and our faces . . .

Yet if I keep walking I won't even manage six miles. In the last three days, with nothing to drink, I have already walked more than a hundred . . .

But as we come to a halt, Prévot says:

'I swear to you there's a lake there.'

'You're crazy!'

'How can it be a mirage at this time, at twilight?'

I don't answer, having long since given up any trust in my eyes. Perhaps it isn't a mirage, but then it's an invention of our madness. How can Prévot go on believing? He persists:

'It's only twenty minutes away, I'm going to have a look . . .'

His stubbornness is getting on my nerves:

'Go and see then, go and take a stroll . . . very good for your health. But let me tell you, if your lake does exist it's salt. And salt or not, it's out in hell somewhere. And it doesn't exist anyway.'

Prévot, staring straight ahead, is already on his way. I know all about these irresistible forces of attraction! And the thought occurs to me: 'There are sleepwalkers who throw themselves straight under trains.' I know that Prévot will not come back. Gripped by the vertigo of empty space, he will not be able to turn around. A little further, and he will fall. And he will die where he is, as I will where I am. How unimportant it all is! . . .

It strikes me that this new indifference in me is a bad omen. When I nearly drowned, I felt the same calmness. But I make use of it to write a posthumous letter, lying flat on some stones. It's a fine letter. Very dignified. Filled with wise and generous advice. Reading it over, I feel a kind of pleasurable conceit. 'What an admirable posthumous letter!' they will say. 'What a pity he's dead!'

I try to take stock of myself. I attempt to form some saliva: how long is it since I spat? No more saliva. If I keep my mouth closed, a sticky substance glues my lips together. It dries, forming a hard crust on the outside of them. Yet I can still manage a swallowing action. And my eyes are not yet filled with bright lights. When I am invited to that shining spectacle, I'll have two hours left.

It's dark now. The moon has grown larger since it last shone. Prévot isn't coming back. Lying on my back, I mull over these self-evident facts. An old sensation is emerging within me, and I am trying to identify it. I am . . . I am . . . on a ship! I was going to

South America, I was stretched out just like this on the upper deck. The tip of the mast was swaying slowly to and fro among the stars. There is no mast here, but I am still on a ship, sailing towards a destination that is independent of my efforts now. Slave traders have bound me and hurled me on to a ship.

I think of Prévot, who isn't coming back. I didn't hear a single complaint from him. That's very good. It would have been unbearable for me to hear any moaning. Prévot is a man.

There he is! Five hundred yards away, waving his torch! He's lost his track! I have no lamp to answer him, so I stand up and shout, but he doesn't hear . . .

A second lamp now, two hundred yards from the first, then a third. My God, a team of beaters, looking for me!

'Hey there!' I shout.

But no one hears.

The three lamps are still signalling.

I am not crazy. I feel fine this evening. I am very calm. I look very carefully. There are three lamps, five hundred yards away.

'Hey!'

But still no one hears.

For the only time, I am gripped for a moment by panic. I can still run, though: 'Wait . . . Wait . . .' They're turning away! They're moving off to look elsewhere, and I can't stand up! I'm going to fall on the threshold of life, when there were arms ready to catch me! . . .

'Hey there! Hey!'

'Hey there! Yes!'

They've heard me. I'm suffocating, I'm suffocating but I'm still running, running towards the voice . . . 'Hey there!' . . . I see Prévot, and I fall to the ground.

'Oh, when I saw all those lights! . . .'

'What lights?'

It's true. He is alone.

This time I feel no despair, just a voiceless anger.

'What about your lake?'

'As I walked forward it moved away. For half an hour I walked towards it. After half an hour it was too far away. I turned back. But I'm sure now that it is a lake . . .'

'You're crazy, completely crazy. Oh, why did you do that? . . . Why?'

What did he do? Why did he do it? I could weep with indignation, but I don't know what I'm indignant about. Prévot, his voice choking in his throat, explains:

'I wanted so much to find something to drink . . . Your lips are so white!'

And my anger dies away . . . I pass my hand over my forehead as if waking from sleep, and I feel a sadness. And gently I tell him:

'As clearly as I see you now, beyond all possible error, I saw three lights . . . I tell you I saw them, Prévot!'

For a time he is silent, then at last he acknowledges:

'Yes. We're in a bad way.'

The earth radiates its heat away swiftly in this atmosphere devoid of moisture. It is already very cold. I stand up and walk about, but soon begin to shiver unbearably. My dehydrated blood is circulating poorly, and I am pierced by an icy chill that is more than just the cold of the night. My jaws are chattering, and my whole body is twitching convulsively. My hand is shaking my torch so much that it has become useless. I who have never been sensitive to cold am about to die of cold. What a strange effect of thirst!

I dropped my waterproof coat somewhere, weary of carrying it in the heat. And little by little the wind is getting worse. And I am discovering that in the desert there is no place of refuge. The desert is as smooth as marble. By day it forms no shade, and at night it delivers you up, naked, to the wind. Not a tree, not a hedge, not a stone that might have sheltered me. The wind is charging at me like a troop of cavalry on open ground. I turn in circles, trying to escape it. I lie down, I get up again. Lying or standing, I am exposed to this icy whip. I cannot run, I have no strength left to flee the assassins, and I fall to my knees with my head in my hands, as the sabre stroke descends!

A little later I realize that I have stood up and am walking straight ahead, still shivering! Where am I? I have set out again, but I hear Prévot! His shouts have brought me to my senses . . .

I come back towards him, still shaking, convulsed through the whole of my body. And I say to myself: 'It isn't the cold. It's something else. It's the end.' I am too dehydrated. I walked so far two days ago, and yesterday on my own.

It grieves me to die of cold. I would rather have my inner visions: that cross, those Arabs, those lamps. It was even becoming interesting. I don't like being whipped like a slave . . .

I'm on my knees again.

We have brought along some medical supplies. A hundred grammes of pure ether, a hundred of 90 per cent alcohol and a small bottle of iodine. I try to drink two or three mouthfuls of the ether. It's like swallowing knives. Then a little of the 90 per cent alcohol, but it contracts my throat.

I dig a pit in the sand, lie down in it, and bury everything but my face. Prévot has found some small sticks and is lighting a fire, but its flames will soon be exhausted. Prévot refuses to bury himself in the sand. He prefers to stamp his feet. He is wrong.

My throat is still constricted, which is a bad sign, and yet I feel better. I feel calm. I feel a calmness beyond all hope. Without meaning to, I am sailing away again, trussed up on the deck of my slave ship under the stars. But perhaps I'm not so very miserable . . .

I no longer feel the cold, provided that I don't move a muscle. And I am forgetting my body as it sleeps under the sand. I shall not move any more, and so I shall suffer nothing more, ever. And in truth, there is little to be suffered . . . Behind all these torments there is the orchestration of fatigue and delirium. And everything is being transformed into a picture-book, into a slightly cruel fairy-story . . . A little while ago the wind was hunting me, and I was running in circles like an animal. Then I had difficulty in breathing: a knee was crushing my chest. A knee. And I struggled against the weight of the angel. Before now I was never alone in the desert. Now that I no longer believe in my surroundings, I am withdrawing into myself, closing my eyes, not moving an eyelash. This great torrent of images is taking me away, I can feel it taking me towards a peaceful dream: the rivers grow calm in the depth of the sea.

Farewell, you whom I loved. It is not my fault if the human body cannot last three days without drinking. I did not believe myself to be such a prisoner of flowing springs, or suspect that independence is so brief. We think man can walk straight ahead, that man is free

. . . We cannot see the rope that attaches him to the well, that binds him like an umbilical cord to the womb of the earth. If he takes one step too many, he dies.

Apart from your suffering, I have no regrets. When all's said and done I've had the best of it. If I could go back, I would start it all again. I need to live. There is no human life in cities now.

Flying is not the point. The aeroplane is a means, not an end. It is not for the plane that we risk our lives. Nor is it for the sake of his plough that the farmer ploughs. But through the plane we can leave the cities and their accountants, and find a truth that farmers know.

We do a man's work and we have a man's worries. We are in contact with the wind, with the stars, with the night, with the sand, with the sea. We try to outwit the forces of nature. We wait for dawn as a gardener waits for spring. We wait for the next port of call as a promised land, and we seek our truth in the stars.

I shall not complain. For three days I have walked, I have been thirsty, I have followed tracks in the sand, I have pinned my hopes on the dew. I have striven to rejoin my kind, whose dwelling-place on the earth I had forgotten. And those are concerns of the living. I cannot but judge them more important than choosing which variety show to go to in the evening.

I can no longer understand those dense crowds on the suburban trains, those men who think they are men and yet who are reduced like ants, by a pressure they do not feel, to the use that is made of them. When they are free, on their absurd little Sundays, how do they fill their time?

Once, in Russia, I heard Mozart being played in a factory. I wrote about it, and received two hundred offensive letters. I have nothing against those who prefer saloon bar honky-tonk, but I do blame the bar-owner. I don't like to see men damaged.

I am happy in my profession. I feel myself to be a ploughman of the skies. In the suburban train, I feel death pangs very different from these! All things considered, this is luxury! . . .

I have no regrets. I've gambled and I've lost. It was all in a day's work. But at least I have breathed the wind of the sea.

That is an unforgettable nourishment for those who have once

tasted it. True, comrades? True. It isn't a matter of living danger-
ously. Such a pretentious phrase. Toreadors don't thrill me. Danger
is not what I love. I know what I love. It is life.

The sky seems about to lighten. I free one arm from the sand and
run my hand over a piece of parachute within my reach. It is dry.
But let's wait. Dew falls at dawn. But dawn lightens the sky, and
there is no moisture on our cloths. My thoughts become a little
blurred, and I hear myself saying: 'There is a dry heart here . . . a
dry heart . . . a dry heart that can form no tears! . . .'

'Come on, Prévot! Our throats are still open: we must keep
walking.'

VII

Now the west wind is blowing, the wind that dries up a man in
nineteen hours. My oesophagus is still not closed, but it is hard and
painful, and I can already sense something rasping in it. That cough
I have heard described will begin soon; I am expecting it. My
tongue is a hindrance. But the worst thing is that I can already see
spots of shining light. When they turn into flames, I will lie down.

We are walking rapidly, taking advantage of the early morning
coolness. We know only too well that when the sun is at its zenith,
as they say, we will walk no further. At its zenith . . .

We have lost the right to sweat. Along with the right to pause.
This coolness is merely the coolness of 18 per cent humidity. This
wind that is blowing comes from the desert, and under its deceitful
and tender caress our blood is evaporating.

On the first day we ate a few grapes. Then, through three days,
half an orange and a fragment of cake. Even if we had food, how
could we swallow it without saliva? But I feel no hunger, only
thirst, and in fact now the effects of thirst rather than thirst itself.
The hard throat, the plaster tongue, the rasping and the foul taste in
the mouth. These are sensations I have never known before. Water
would cure them, no doubt, but nothing in my memory associates
them with that remedy. Thirst is becoming more and more a
sickness, less and less a craving.

Images of springs and fruits already seem less heartbreaking. I am forgetting the radiance of the orange, as I seem to have forgotten my affections. Perhaps my memory is already empty.

We have sat down, but we must keep going. No more long stretches now. Every five hundred yards we collapse with fatigue, and lying down is bliss. But we must keep going.

The landscape is changing. The stones are more sparse, and we are walking on sand. There are dunes a mile ahead, with some patches of stunted vegetation. I prefer the sand to the steely armour. I prefer the golden desert. The Sahara. I seem to recognize it . . .

Now two hundred yards are enough to exhaust us.

'But we're going to make it to those bushes, if that's all we ever do.'

That is the final limit. A week later, when we come back over our tracks in a car to search for the Simoun, we will confirm that our last effort took us fifty miles. So I have already done about a hundred and twenty. How could I carry on?

Yesterday I was walking without hope. Today those words have lost their meaning. Today we are walking because we are walking. Like oxen ploughing, I imagine. Yesterday I dreamed of a paradise of orange groves. Today, for me, there is no paradise. I do not believe the orange groves exist.

There is nothing more within me but a heart squeezed totally dry. I shall fall, and I acknowledge no despair. No suffering, even. This I regret, for sorrow would be as sweet as water. It would bring pity, compassion for myself as from a friend. But I have no friend in the world now.

When they find me, with my eyes burnt out, they will imagine that I must have cried out and suffered greatly. But surges of emotion, regrets and sweet sufferings are all forms of wealth, and I have no more wealth. Pure young girls know sorrow as their first love fades into its evening, and they weep. Sorrow is linked to the vibrant rhythm of life. And I have no more sorrow . . .

I am the desert. I can form no more saliva, but neither can I form the tender images that would call forth moans of grief. The sun has dried up the well of tears within me.

And yet, what have I just seen? A breath of hope has passed over me like a breeze rippling the sea. What sign has just awakened my instinct before striking my conscious mind? Nothing has changed, and yet everything has changed. This sheet of sand, these mounds and these sparse patches of greenery are no longer a landscape, but a setting. The stage is still empty, but the scene is set. I look at Prévot. The same amazement has struck him, but he too has no grasp of what he is experiencing.

I swear to you that something is about to happen . . .

I swear to you that the desert has come alive. I swear to you that this absence and this silence are suddenly more filled with stirring life than a square packed with people . . .

We are saved, there are tracks in the sand! . . .

We had lost the trail of the human species, we were cut off from our tribe, we had found ourselves alone in the world, left behind by the universal movement of men, and here now we discover, marked in the sand, their miraculous footprints.

'Look, Prévot, here two men separated . . .'

'Here a camel knelt down . . .'

'And here . . .'

But we are not saved yet. We cannot simply wait. In a few hours we will be past help. Once the cough sets in, thirst's onslaught is too swift. And our throats . . .

Yet I believe in that caravan, as it sways along somewhere, in the desert.

So we walked on, and suddenly I heard a cock crow. Guillaumet told me: 'Towards the end, I heard cocks crowing in the Andes. I heard railway trains too . . .'

I remember his story the instant the cock crows here, and tell myself:

'My eyes were the first to deceive me. It must be an effect of thirst. My ears have held out longer . . .' But Prévot grips my arm:

'Did you hear it?'

'What?'

'The cock crowing!'

'So . . . then . . .'

Yes, of course, you fool, it's life . . .

I had one final hallucination: three dogs chasing each other. Prévot was looking, but he couldn't see them. But there are two of us, stretching out our arms towards the Bedouin. There are two of us dragging every ounce of breath from our lungs. Two of us, laughing with joy! . . .

But our voices won't carry thirty yards. Our vocal chords have dried up. We've been speaking to each other in whispers, without knowing it!

The Bedouin and his camel have just appeared from behind the dune, but now, now they are slowly beginning to move away. Perhaps this man is alone. A cruel demon has shown him to us only to withdraw him from our sight . . .

And how could we run now?

Another Arab appears in profile on the dune. We shout, but it is no more than a whisper. So we wave our arms, as if filling the sky with giant signals. But the Bedouin is still gazing to the right . . .

And now he begins a leisurely quarter-turn. At the instant when he faces us head-on, the miracle will be accomplished. The very instant when he looks in our direction will itself obliterate thirst, death and mirages. He has made his quarter-turn, and the world has already changed. Merely a movement of his upper body, merely a shift in his gaze will create life, and to me he looks like a god . . .

It is a miracle . . . He is walking towards us over the sand, like a god on the surface of the sea . . .

The Arab simply looked at us. He placed his hands firmly on our shoulders, and we obeyed him. We lay down upon the sand. There are no races here, nor any languages, nor any discord . . . There is this poor nomad who has placed his archangelic hands on our shoulders.

We waited, our foreheads on the sand. And now we are drinking, flat on our stomachs, heads in the bowl like calves. The Bedouin is alarmed, and keeps making us pause. But as soon as he lets us go our faces plunge back into the water.

Water!

Water, you have neither taste, nor colour, nor scent. You cannot be defined. You are savoured, but you remain unknown. You are not a necessity of life: you are life. You fill us with a joy that is not of the senses. You restore to us all powers we had surrendered. Through your grace, all the desiccated springs of our hearts flow forth once more.

Of all the riches in the world you are the greatest, and the most delicate, you who lie so pure in the womb of the earth. A man can die by a magnesian spring. He can die a yard from a salt lake. He can die in spite of a quart of dew with chemicals suspended in it. You can accept no mixing, bear no adulteration; you are a sensitive divinity . . .

But you spread within us an infinitely simple happiness.

Yet as for you, our saviour, Bedouin of Libya, you will be for ever effaced from my memory. I will never be able to remember your face. You are Man, and you appear to me with the face of all men together. You have never set eyes on us, yet you have recognized us. You are our beloved brother. And I in my turn will recognize you in all men.

Bathed in a light of nobility and generosity you appear before me, great Lord with the power to give water to drink. All my friends and all my enemies are walking towards me in your person, and I have no enemy left in all the world.

VIII

MEN

I

Once again I have rubbed shoulders with a truth without fully comprehending it. I thought I was lost for ever, I thought I had reached the bottom of the pit of despair, and then with renunciation I knew peace. It seems that at such times we discover ourselves and become our own friend. Nothing can break down that sense of completeness, that fulfilment within us of some fundamental need unknown until that moment. I imagine that Bonnafous, as he rode to exhaustion before the wind, knew that serenity. Guillaumet too, in his snowfield. And how could I forget that as I lay buried in sand up to my neck, with thirst slowly slitting my throat, I felt such warmth in my heart under my cloak of stars?

How can we give such a sense of deliverance its full value within us? We all know what a paradoxical creature man is. You give a man his daily bread so that he can be creative and he just goes to sleep; the victorious conqueror grows soft, the magnanimous man turns miser as he gains in wealth. Of what value to us are those political doctrines that proclaim a new blossoming of mankind, if we do not know at the outset what kind of man they will bring forth? Who will be born? We are not cattle to be fattened for market, and the birth of a Pascal in poverty carries more weight than the arrival of any number of prosperous nonentities.

We cannot foresee what is most essential. Each of us has experienced the most blazing joys with no forewarning of their coming. We remember them with such yearning that we are nostalgic even for our sufferings, if it was our sufferings that gave them birth. All of us, meeting old friends again, have tasted the magic of bad memories.

What do we know, except that there are mysterious circumstances that make us fruitful? Where is man's reality to be found?

Truth is not in that which can be demonstrated. If orange trees put down firm roots and bear fruit in one piece of ground and not in another, that piece of ground is truth for orange trees. If a particular religion, culture, scale of values and pattern of activities encourage that sense of fulfilment in man, liberating within him a lord who was oblivious to his own sovereignty, then that culture, that scale of values and those activities are the truth of man. And logic? Let it cobble together what explanation it can for life.

All through this book I have held up as models some of those who seem to me to have obeyed a sovereign vocation, who chose the desert or the airline as others would have chosen the monastery; but I have betrayed my purpose if I have aroused principally in you an admiration for men themselves. What is admirable above all is the ground in which they have their foundations.

Vocation plays a part, certainly. Some men stay closeted in their little shops. Others travel with urgency on a necessary road: in the story of their childhood we find the seeds of the impulses that will explain their destiny. But History, read after the event, is an illusion. Those impulses could be found in almost every man. We have all known shopkeepers who, in some night of fire or shipwreck, have been revealed as greater than themselves. They have no illusions about the quality of their fulfilment: that fire is and will remain the night of their life. But for want of fresh opportunities, for want of favourable ground, for want of a demanding religion, they have returned to their sleep without believing in their own greatness. A sense of vocation helps man to liberate himself, certainly: but it is just as necessary to liberate the vocation.

Nights in the air, nights in the desert . . . those are rare opportunities, offered to few men. And yet, when circumstances bring them to life, all men reveal the same needs. I shall not digress if I tell the story of a night in Spain which taught me this. Having spoken too much of some men, I would like now to speak of all.

It was on the Madrid front. I was there as a reporter. I was eating supper that night deep in an underground shelter, at the table of a young captain.

II

As we were talking the telephone rang, and now a long dialogue is under way. HQ is ordering a local attack in that working-class suburb, an absurd and desperate attack with the objective of knocking out some houses that have been turned into concrete fortresses. The captain turns back towards us, shrugging his shoulders: 'The first of us to show his face . . .' he says, and then he pushes two glasses of brandy towards a sergeant and me:

'You'll go first, with me,' he tells the sergeant. 'Drink that, and get some sleep.'

The sergeant has gone to get some sleep. There are ten of us awake around the table. In that meticulously blacked-out room the harshness of the light is making me blink. Five minutes ago, I glanced out through a loophole. Pulling aside the cloth that covered it, I saw ruined, haunted houses, drowned in a chasm of moonlight. As I replaced the cloth it seemed to wipe away the moonbeam like a splash of oil. In my eyes now I still have that image of glaucous fortresses.

These soldiers will probably not come back, but a sense of propriety keeps them silent. The coming attack is in the order of things. Drawing on a stock of men. Drawing on a seed store. A handful of seeds for sowing.

And we drink our brandy. To my right, a game of chess. Jokes to my left. Where am I? A semi-drunken man makes his entrance, stroking a shaggy beard and rolling affectionate eyes at us. His gaze falls on the brandy, moves away, comes back to the brandy, and swings in supplication to the captain, who laughs quietly. As hope dawns, the man laughs too, and laughter ripples gently through the watchers. The captain pulls back the bottle a little, the man's eyes feign despair, and so a childish game begins. Through the dense cigarette smoke, through the fatigue of that sleepless night and the vision of the coming attack, this silent ballet has the quality of a dream.

And we play, enclosed in the warmth of the hold of our ship, while explosions are intensifying outside, like a crashing sea swell.

In a little while these men will cleanse themselves of their sweat, their alcohol, all the dirt of their waiting, in the alchemical waters of the night of war. I can sense how close they are to purification. But still they are dancing, for as long as they can dance it, the ballet of the drunkard and the bottle. Playing the chess game for as long as they can play it. Making life last as long as they can. But high on a shelf they have set an alarm-clock, and it will ring. And then these men will stand up, stretch themselves, and buckle on their ammunition-belts. The captain will take his revolver from its holster. The drunkard will be sober. And without undue haste they will enter that corridor that slopes gently up to a blue rectangle of night sky. They will say something simple like: 'Bloody stupid attack . . .' or: 'God, it's cold.' And then they will plunge.

I was there when they woke the sergeant. He was sleeping on an iron bed, in the ruins of a cellar. I watched him as he slept. He seemed to be enjoying a sleep without anguish, a happy sleep. He reminded me of that first day in Libya, when Prévot and I, stranded without water and condemned to die but not yet suffering too acute a thirst, were able to sleep, just once, for two hours at a stretch. As I fell asleep I had the sense of a remarkable power at my disposal: the power to reject the present. The body I owned was not tormenting me as yet, and so once I had buried my face in my arms there was no distinction, for me, between that night and a happy night.

The sergeant was at rest in just that way, curled up, without human shape, and when those who came to wake him had lit a candle and stuck it into the neck of a bottle, nothing emerged clearly from the shapeless mass at first except a pair of boots. Huge, hobnailed, iron-clad boots, the boots of a farm labourer or a stevedore.

This man was shod in the tools of his trade, and his body bore them everywhere: cartridge pouches, revolvers, leather straps, ammunition belt. He was wearing the packsaddle, the collar, the entire harness of the plough horse. Deep in caves, in Morocco, you can see mill-stones turned by blind horses. Here too, in the flickering, reddish light of the candle, we were waking a blind horse so that he could turn his mill-stone.

'Hey, Sergeant!'

Slowly he stirred, revealing his sleeping face and muttering something unintelligible, then turned back to the wall, unwilling to wake up, plunging back into the deep waters of sleep as if into the peace of his mother's womb, grasping with his opening and closing fists at some unknown black seaweed. We had to loosen his fingers. We sat on his bed, and one of us placed an arm gently behind his neck and greeted that heavy head with a smile as he lifted it. It was as if two horses were gently stroking each other's neck in a warm stable. 'Come on, comrade!' I have never seen anything more loving in my life. The sergeant tried one last time to return to his happy dreams, to reject our world of dynamite, of exhaustion and freezing nights, but it was too late. Something had come from outside, a call to duty, as a schoolboy in disgrace is awakened slowly by the school bell on a Sunday. Desk, blackboard and extra work forgotten, he was dreaming of playing in the countryside; in vain. The bell is still ringing, bringing him inexorably back within the scope of man's injustice. Just like him, little by little and unwillingly, the sergeant was taking responsibility for his fatigue-worn body, that body which would soon be racked with joint pain in the early morning cold and then would know the weight of the harness, the lumbering run, and death. Not so much death as the sticky pool of blood soaking his hands in his effort to rise, the cramped breathing, the coldness all around; not so much death as the discomfort of dying. As I watched him I was still thinking of the desolation of my own awakening, of taking on once more the burden of thirst, of sunlight, of sand, the burden of life, this dream that we have not chosen.

But now he is standing, looking us in the eye:

'Is it time?'

This is the point where man becomes visible. Where he escapes the expectations of logic. The sergeant was smiling! What can this temptation be? I remember a night in Paris when Mermoz and I had been celebrating some birthday or other with friends. At daybreak we found ourselves in the doorway of a bar, nauseated from too much talk, too much drink, a weariness without purpose. But with the sky already growing light, Mermoz suddenly gripped my arm so fiercely that I felt his nails: 'Look, it's that time. In Dakar now . . .' It was the time when the mechanics rub their eyes and pull off the propeller covers, when the pilot goes to check the weather forecast, when the earth is peopled only by comrades. Colour was already filling the sky, a feast was already being prepared, the cloth being spread; but it was for others, we were not the guests. Others would be taking their chance with danger . . .

'What a lousy dump this is . . .' Mermoz concluded.

And what about you, sergeant, what invitation to a banquet did you have that was worth dying for?

I already knew your secrets. You had told me your story. You were a book-keeper somewhere in Barcelona, drawing up columns of figures without much concern for the divisions within your country. But one friend joined up, then another, then a third, and you experienced to your surprise a strange transformation: little by little, your daily concerns came to seem futile to you. Your pleasures, your worries and your petty comforts all belonged to another time. But still that was not the essence of it. At last one day there came the news that one of your colleagues had been killed near Malaga. He wasn't a friend whose death you might have wanted to avenge; as for politics, you'd never bothered with it. And yet that news swept over you, and over the destinies you shared so closely, like a wind from the sea. A friend looked at you that morning:

'Are we in?'

'We're in.'

And 'in' you were.

Images came to me to clarify a truth which you could not put into words, yet whose self-evidence governed your action.

When the wild ducks pass in the migrating season, they cause strange tides to rise in the lands beneath them. As if magnetized by the great triangular flock, the farmyard ducks try clumsily to leave the ground. The call of the wild has awakened some vestige of the wild within them, and for a moment they have turned into birds of passage. In those hard little heads normally filled with simple images of the pond, of worms and of their roosting-house, now stretch the vast continents, the taste of the ocean winds and the shape of the seas. The creature never knew until now that its brain could contain such marvels, and it beats its wings in contempt for seed and worms, trying to become a wild duck.

But above all it was my gazelles that came into my mind; I kept gazelles at Juby. Everyone did. We enclosed them within a trellis fence, in the open air because they need the running water of the wind, and because nothing is as fragile as a gazelle. Captured young, they survive nevertheless, and they take food from your hand. You can stroke them, and they push their damp muzzle into your palm, and you think they are tame. You think you have sheltered them from that unknown sorrow that silently snuffs out their flame, bringing the softest of deaths to gazelles ... But the day comes when you find them pushing the fence with their horns, looking towards the desert, drawn by a magnet. Escape from you is not their conscious thought. They come to drink the milk you bring them, and press their muzzle even more affectionately into your palm ... But as soon as you let them go, you find that after the brief semblance of a contented gallop they are pressed against the fence once more. And unless you intervene again they stay there, not struggling against the barrier but simply pressing their horns against it with lowered heads, and they would stay there until they died. Is it the mating season, or just the need to gallop until they have no breath left? They do not know. Their eyes were not even open when you took them captive. They know nothing of freedom amid the sands, nor of the scent of the male. But you have greater intelligence, and you know what they are seeking: the vast open space that will fulfil them. They want to become gazelles and dance their dance. They want to experience the straight sprint at eighty miles an hour, punctuated by abrupt leaps as if flames were springing at them from the sand. Jackals have little importance if truth for gazelles is to taste fear, if it is fear alone that makes them surpass themselves, driving them to the most spectacular acrobatics! What does the lion matter if truth for gazelles is to be ripped open by a claw in the sunlight? You watch them, and you think they feel a yearning. Yearning, a desire for something unnameable ... The object of desire exists, but there are no words to express it.

And what about us? What do we yearn for?

What might you find here, sergeant, to make you feel that you were no longer betraying your destiny? Perhaps it was that brotherly arm raising your sleeping head, perhaps that affectionate smile, a smile of sharing rather than pity? 'Come on, comrade ...' Pity implies two people, divided still. But at a certain altitude in relationships gratitude and pity lose their meaning, and you can breathe like a released prisoner.

We experienced that oneness when we were flying over Rio de Oro, still rebel territory then, in two planes. I never heard the victim thank his rescuer. Most of the time we insulted each other, in fact, all through the exhausting transfer of mail bags from one plane to the other: 'Stupid bastard! If my engine's broken down it's your fault, you and your mania for flying at seven thousand feet straight into a head wind! If you'd stayed low behind me we'd be at Port-Étienne by now!' . . . and the other, offering up his life, felt shame that he had been that bastard. What would we have thanked him for anyway? He had a right to our life just as we did, for we were branches of the same tree. And I felt a pride in you, my rescuer!

Why, sergeant, would the man who prepared you for death have pitied you? You were all facing that danger for each other. That moment reveals a oneness that needs no language. I understood you as you set out. Though you had been poor in Barcelona, perhaps alone after your day's work, with no refuge even for your body, here you experienced a sense of fulfilment as you became part of universality: you, the outcast, were brought within love.

Were they sincere, were they logical, the politicians' speeches which may have sown the seed in you? I don't give a damn. If they took hold in you like ripening seed, it is because they responded to your needs. Only you can judge. Only the soil can recognize the corn.

III

Once we are bound to our brothers by a common goal that is outside us, then we can breathe. Experience teaches us that to love is not to gaze at one another but to gaze together in the same direction. There is no comradeship except through unity on the same rope, climbing towards the same peak. If that were not the case, then why, in the century of material comfort, would we experience such overflowing joy at sharing our last rations in the desert? What value do sociologists' forecasts have when set against that? All other pleasures seem trivial to those of us who have known the joy of a rescue in the Sahara.

Perhaps that is why the world today is beginning to crack apart around us. Everyone seems inspired by some religion that promises fulfilment. Within the clashing words we are all expressing the same impulses. We are divided over methods which are the fruit of our reasonings, but not over our goals, which are identical.

Let nothing astonish us from now on. The man who had no notion of the stranger sleeping within him, but who sensed his awakening at a single moment in an anarchists' cellar in Barcelona, will know only one truth, through sacrifice, through mutual support, through an inflexible vision of justice: the truth of the anarchists. And as for the man who, just once, stands guard to protect a whole congregation of little nuns as they kneel in terror in a Spanish convent, that man will die for the Church.

If you had put it to Mermoz, as he plunged towards the Chilean face of the Andes with victory in his heart, that he was wrong, that no business letter was worth the risk of his life, Mermoz would have laughed in your face. Truth is the man who was born in Mermoz as he flew through the Andes.

If you want to convince a willing fighter of the horror of war, don't call him a barbarian: try to understand him before judging him.

Consider that officer in South Morocco, who at the time of the Rif war was commanding an outpost, hemmed in between two mountains held by rebels. One evening, he was visited by a delegation from the western mountain. They were drinking tea, as was the custom, when a volley of shots rang out. The tribes from the eastern mountain were attacking the post. The captain tried to move the enemy delegation out, but they replied: 'Today we are your guests. God will not allow us to desert you . . .' And so they joined his men and saved the post, before climbing back to their eyrie.

But the day before their own assault was due, they sent ambassadors to the captain:

'We came to your aid the other day . . .'

'That's true.'

'For you we used up three hundred cartridges . . .'

'That's true.'

'It would be an act of justice to return them to us.'

The captain was a gentleman. He could not exploit an advantage gained from their generosity of spirit. He gave them the cartridges that would be used against him.

Truth for a man is what makes him a man. When a man has experienced this dignity in relationships, this loyalty when the stakes are high, this mutual gift of esteem within matters of life and death, when he compares this ennoblement granted to him with the mediocre bonhomie of the demagogue who would have expressed his fraternity with those same Arabs by clapping them heartily on the shoulders, flattering them yet at the same time humiliating them, then that man will feel towards you merely a slightly contemptuous pity if you argue against him. And he will be right.

But you will be equally right to hate war.

If your purpose is to understand man and his needs, to know what is most essential about him, you must not set the proof of one man's truth against another's. Yes, you are right. Everyone is right. Anything can be demonstrated by logic. The man who blames the ills of this world on hunchbacks is right. Let's declare war on hunchbacks, and all get carried away. We'll avenge the crimes of the hunchbacks. And yes, hunchbacks do commit crimes.

In the effort to identify what is essential, we need to forget for a moment the divisions which, once they are accepted, bring with them a whole Koran of unshakeable truths and the fanaticism that they spawn. You can line men up as right wing and left wing, hunchbacks and non-hunchbacks, fascists and democrats, and those distinctions are unassailable. But truth, as we know, is that which simplifies the world and not that which creates chaos. Truth is the language that identifies what is universal. Newton did not 'discover' a law long hidden like the answer to a rebus; Newton carried out a creative operation. He founded a human language which could express simultaneously the falling of an apple in a meadow and the rising of the sun. Truth is not that which can be demonstrated, it is that which simplifies.

There is no purpose in discussing ideologies. They can all be demonstrated and yet be set against each other, and such discussions bring us only despair for the salvation of mankind, while all around us men themselves display the same needs.

We want to be set free. The man driving a pickaxe into the ground wants to know the meaning of his pickaxe blow. The pickaxe blow of the convict, a humiliation for the convict, is not the same as the pickaxe blow of the prospector, which gives stature to the prospector. Prison is not in the place where the pickaxe blows fall. The horror is not physical. Prison is where pickaxe blows fall without purpose, fall without bonding the man to the community of men.

And we yearn to escape from that prison.

There are two hundred million men in Europe who have no sense of purpose and who yearn to be born. Industry has torn them from the language of their rural lineage, and has imprisoned them in vast ghettos like marshalling yards congested with trains of black wagons. Deep within their slums, they yearn to be awakened.

There are others, caught in the cogwheels of their trades, who are forbidden the joys of the pioneer, the religious man or the scientist. Once it was thought sufficient to clothe and feed them, to satisfy their needs. And little by little the petit bourgeois characters of Courteline's plays took root in them: the village politician, the technician devoid of any inner life. They receive a good training, but they receive no culture. The man who believes that culture consists in the memorizing of formulae has a paltry notion of culture. A third-rate mathematics student knows more about nature and its laws than did Pascal or Descartes. Is he capable of the same agility of thought?

All of us, in ways more or less obscure, feel the need to be born. But there are deceptive solutions. You can certainly bring men to life by putting them in uniform. They will sing their war psalms and break bread together as comrades. They will have found what they are seeking, a taste of universality. But of the bread they are given they will die.

You can dig up wooden idols and revive tried and tested old myths that have served for better or for worse, you can resuscitate the mysticism of Pan-Germanism or the Holy Roman Empire. You can intoxicate the Germans with the intoxication of being German and compatriots of Beethoven. You can make them drunk with it right down to the stoker in the coal-bunker. It's certainly easier than bringing a Beethoven out of the stoker.

But such idols are carnivorous idols. The man who dies for the progress of knowledge or the healing of diseases is serving life even as he dies. It may be a fine thing to die for the expansion of territory, but today war destroys what it claims to foster. It isn't a matter now of sacrificing a little blood to invigorate the whole race. Now that it is waged with the aeroplane and with poison gas, war is nothing more than a bloody surgery. Each side settles behind a concrete wall, and for want of a better idea hurls out squadrons night after night to torpedo the entrails of the other, to blow its vital centres apart, to paralyse its production and its trade. The winner is the one who decomposes last. And they decompose together.

In a world turned to desert, we thirsted for comradeship: the taste of bread broken among comrades made us accept the values of war. But we do not need war to feel the warmth of neighbouring shoulders as we head for the same goal. War deceives us. Hatred adds nothing to the excitement of the journey.

Why hate one another? We stand together, carried along by the same planet, the crew of a single ship. If it is good that civilizations compete to promote new syntheses, it is monstrous that they devour one another.

To set us free, it is enough that we help each other to become aware of a goal which binds us one to another, so why not seek it in unity? The surgeon on his rounds is not listening to the patient as he sounds his chest: beyond those moanings he is seeking a cure for man himself. The surgeon speaks a universal language, as does the physicist when he contemplates those almost divine equations through which he can grasp both the atom and the nebula. And so it is with the humblest shepherd watching modestly over a few sheep beneath the stars, for if he is aware of the part he is playing he will discover that he is more than a servant. He is a sentinel. And each sentinel is responsible for the whole empire.

Do you really believe that the shepherd does not want that aware-

ness? On the Madrid front I visited a school that had been set up
five hundred yards from the trenches, behind a little stone wall on a
hillside. A corporal was teaching botany. As his hands separated the
fragile elements of a poppy, he drew towards him bearded pilgrims
who came out of the surrounding mud, climbing on a pilgrimage
towards him despite the falling shells. Gathered around the corporal
and sitting cross-legged, they listened with their chins resting on
their fists. They frowned and clenched their teeth, understanding
little of the lesson, but someone had said to them: 'You're just
brutes hardly out of your caves, try joining the human race!' . . .
and they stumped quickly up here to join it.

Only when we become aware of the part we play, even the most
unobtrusive part, will we be happy. Only then will we live in peace
and die in peace, for what gives meaning to life gives meaning to
death.

Death is sweet when it is in the order of things, when the old
Provençal peasant, at the end of his reign, entrusts to his sons his
plot of land with its goats and olive trees, in order that they may
hand it on in their turn to the sons of their sons. In the rural lineage
death is only half a death. Each existence cracks in its turn like a
pod, and gives up its seeds.

I once stood by three countrymen at the deathbed of their
mother. There was grief, of course. For the second time the
umbilical cord was cut. For the second time, the knot that binds
two generations was unfastened. Those three sons were discovering
that they were alone, with everything to learn, with no family table
now where they could meet at festivals, with no pole of self-
recognition. But in that moment of severance I was also discovering
that life can be granted for a second time. Each of these sons
would in turn become the head of a family, a rallying-point and a
patriarch, until the time when they in turn would pass on the
leadership to that little group of children now playing outside the
door.

I looked at the mother, that old peasant with her firm and
peaceful face, with her tight lips and her face that was now a mask
of stone. And I saw in it the faces of the sons. That mask had

served to mould their faces. That body had served to mould their bodies, those fine examples of men. And now she lay there broken, but like a matrix after the precious metal has been extracted. Sons and daughters in their turn would mould children in the image of their flesh. No one died on that farm. The mother is dead, long live the mother!

There was grief, yes, but that picture of the lineage is so clear and simple. On its way it casts off those white-haired outer skins one by one, as it travels on towards its own unknowable truth, through all its metamorphoses.

That is why the knell tolling in the little country village that evening seemed filled not with despair but with a discreet and tender rejoicing. That bell which celebrated burials and baptisms with the same voice was now announcing one more passage from a generation to the next. It sang the betrothal of a poor old woman and the earth, and as I listened it gave me only a sense of great peace.

What was being thus transmitted from generation to generation, at the slow pace of a tree's growth, was life itself, but it was also consciousness. An ascension filled with mystery! From flowing lava, from the unformed substance of a star, from a miraculously germinated living cell we have emerged and have risen little by little until we can write cantatas and weigh galaxies.

The mother had not merely passed on life: she had taught her sons a language, entrusted to them the stock of knowledge so slowly gathered through the centuries, the spiritual patrimony that she herself had received in trust, the parcel of traditions, concepts and myths that are the whole of the difference between the brute in his cave and Shakespeare or Newton.

What we feel when we are hungry, with that hunger which drove Spanish soldiers under fire to a botany lesson, which drove Mermoz towards the south Atlantic, which drives another man to write his poem, is that the genesis of man is not yet accomplished and that we must become fully aware of ourselves and of the universe. We must throw out bridges into the darkness. The only ones among us who do not know this are those who affect an indifference they call egoism, and take it for wisdom; but everything in the world refutes that wisdom! Comrades, my comrades, I call you as witnesses: when did we feel happy?

IV

And now, as I reach the final pages of this book, I remember those ageing civil servants who served as our escort at dawn on the day of our first mail flight, as we who had been fortunate to be called prepared for our transformation into men. And yet they were like us, but did not know that they were hungry.

Too many men are left sleeping.

A few years ago, during a long railway journey, I felt the need to explore the country on wheels in which I was locked for three days, a prisoner for three days of that sound like shingle rolled by the sea, and I rose to my feet. At about one in the morning I walked the length of the train. The sleeping cars were empty. The first-class carriages were empty.

But the third-class held hundreds of Polish workers. They were being sent home from France. I stepped over sleeping bodies in the corridors, and stopped to look. I could see, in the glow of the night-lights in an undivided wagon that looked and smelled like a barrack-room or a police station, a whole confused mass of people churned by the swaying of the train. A whole people deep in its bad dreams, returning to its wretchedness. Great shaven heads tilted on the wood of the seats. Men, women and children, all turning from side to side as if assaulted by all those noises, all those joltings that threatened them in their oblivion. They had been denied the hospitality of sound sleep.

And as I looked, they seemed in part to have lost their human quality, tossed as they were from one end of Europe to the other by economic currents, torn away from their little houses in northern France with their tiny gardens and the three pots of geraniums that I had seen in Polish miners' windows. They had gathered together just their cooking utensils, blankets and curtains, in crudely tied and bursting bundles. They had been forced to sacrifice everything they had caressed or charmed, everything they had succeeded in taming

117

in their four or five years in France, the cat and the dog and the geranium, and had brought with them just pots and pans.

A child sucked at the breast of a mother so weary that she seemed asleep. Life was being passed on amid the absurdity and the disorder of this journey. I looked at the father. A heavy skull, naked as a stone. A body hunched in uncomfortable sleep, imprisoned in working clothes, all bumps and hollows. That man was like a lump of wet earth, like those shapeless wrecks that lie heavily on market benches at night. And I thought: the problem is not in this poverty, nor in this filth, nor in this ugliness. But this same man and this same woman met one day, and the man probably smiled at the woman: after his day's work he probably brought her flowers. Timid and awkward, afraid perhaps of rejection. But perhaps the woman, sure of her charms and through natural coquetry, enjoyed his insecurity. And the man, who today is no more than a machine for swinging a pick or a hammer, felt the delicious anguish of love in his heart. The mystery is that they should have become these lumps of wet earth. Through what terrible mould were they forced, to be marked by it as if by a stamping machine? An old animal still has its grace. How can this beautiful human clay be so ravaged?

I travelled on amid this nation, amid their sleep that was as murky as a den of vice. Around them hovered a sound made up of rasping snores, dull moans, and the scraping of boots as men crushed on one side turned to try the other. And always that muted, endless accompaniment of shingle rolled by the sea.

I sat down opposite one couple. Between the man and the woman the child had hollowed out some sort of space, and he was sleeping. He turned as he slept, and I saw his face in the glow of the night-light. What an adorable face! That couple had brought forth a kind of golden fruit. Out of these heavy old rags had come forth a masterpiece of charm and grace. I bent over that smooth brow, that soft pout of the lips, and said to myself: this is a musician's face, this is Mozart as a child, this face promises a life filled with beauty. Little princes in legends were just like him: protected, cultivated, the object of attention, what might he not become? When by mutation a new rose is born in a garden, all the gardeners are stirred. They isolate the rose, tend the rose and foster its growth. But for men there is no gardener. This child Mozart will be marked like the others by the stamping machine. This Mozart will find his greatest pleasure in tenth-rate music, in the stench of cheap dance-halls. This Mozart is condemned.

I went back to my carriage, telling myself: the fate of those people causes them little suffering. And it is not charity that is tormenting me, not an urge to weep over an endlessly reopened wound. Those who carry the wound do not feel it. It is in effect the human race, and not the individual, that is wounded here, wronged here. I have little or no belief in pity. What torments me is the gardener's point of view. What torments me is not this poverty in which, after all, a man can settle just as he can in idleness. Generations of Orientals live contentedly in filth. What torments me will not be cured by soup kitchens. What torments me is not these hollows nor these humps, nor this ugliness, but a part of the murder of Mozart in every one of these men.

Only the Spirit, breathing upon the clay, can create Man.

PENGUIN MODERN CLASSICS

SOUTHERN MAIL/ NIGHT FLIGHT

ANTOINE DE SAINT-EXUPÉRY

'Some of the finest prose written this century, lyrical, at times visionary, polished and still fresh' *Spectator*

Antoine de Saint-Exupéry, an intrepid and eccentric adventurer, transferred his passion for flying to the written word by writing several classics of aviation literature, including *Southern Mail* and *Night Flight*. Based on Saint-Exupéry's trail-blazing flights for the French airmail service over the Sahara and, later, the Andes, these two novels evoke the tragic courage and nobility of the airborne pioneers who took enormous risk, flying in open cock-pits in planes that were often fragile and unstable.

'Saint-Exupéry evokes a sublime world, far from the dismal cares of earth, where man might find his true self in the reverie of flight' *Daily Telegraph*

Translated by Curtis Cate
With a Preface to *Night Flight* by André Gide

PENGUIN MODERN CLASSICS

THE LITTLE PRINCE
ANTOINE DE SAINT-EXUPÉRY

With *Letter to a Hostage*

'An entirely original fable, brilliantly walking a tightrope over the whimsical'
Naomi Lewis, *Independent on Sunday*

Moral allegory and spiritual autobiography, *The Little Prince* is the most translated
book in the French language. With a timeless charm it tells the story of a little
boy who leaves the safety of his own tiny planet to travel the universe, learning
the vagaries of adult behaviour through a series of extraordinary encounters. His
personal odyssey culminates in a voyage to Earth and further adventures.

Letter to a Hostage, which contains certain themes that were to appear in *The
Little Prince*, is Saint-Exupéry's optimistic and humane open letter to a Jewish
intellectual hiding in occupied France in 1943.

'[It is] resonant, beautiful and the kind of book that you should slip into an inside
pocket to peek at for the rest of your life' *Guardian* on *Letter to a Hostage*

Translated with an Introduction by T. V. F. Cuffe

PENGUIN MODERN CLASSICS

WINTER'S TALES
ISAK DINESEN (KAREN BLIXEN)

'Tales as delicate as Venetian glass' *The New York Times*

After the huge success of her autobiography *Out of Africa*, Isak Dinesen returned to a European setting in these exquisite, rapturous tales of rebirth and redemption.

Beginning with a sailor boy's bold progression into manhood, these stories are full of longing, a theme often mirrored in the desire to escape to sea, as in 'The Young Man with the Carnation' and 'Peter and Rosa'. This collection also includes 'Snow-Acre', a modern rendition of a folk-tale in which old ideals clash with the new order, and is considered by many to be one of her finest stories. Full of psychological insights, these luminous tales reveal the mystery and unexpectedness of human behaviour.

PENGUIN MODERN CLASSICS

THE SHELTERING SKY
PAUL BOWLES

'A novel touched with genius ... a book of challenging power and penetration, a story of almost unbearable tensions' *Evening Standard*

After ten years of marriage, Kit and Port Moresby have drifted apart and are sexually estranged. Avoiding the chaos of Europe in the aftermath of the Second World War, they travel to the remote North African desert. Port hopes the journey will reunite them, but although they share similar emotions, they are divided by their conflicting outlooks on life. Kit fears the desert while Port is drawn to its beauty and remoteness. Oblivious to its dangers, he falls ill and they discover a hostile, violent world that threatens to destroy them both.

With an Introduction by Michael Hofmann